THE OUTER PATH

Finding my way in Tibet

Jim Reynolds

Edited by Kathleen Hallam

Foreword by the Dalai Lama

Fair Oaks Publishing
Sunnyvale, California

Book design and maps by Susan Cronin-Paris

Published by Fair Oaks Publishing
941 Populus Place
Sunnyvale, CA 94086
(408) 732-1078

Library of Congress Cataloging-in-Publication Data

Reynolds, Jim, 1962-
    The outer path : finding my way in Tibet / Jim Reynolds ;
edited by Kathleen Hallam ; foreword by the Dalai Lama.
        p.   cm.
    ISBN 0-933271-06-9 (pbk. : alk. paper) : $10.95
    1. Tibet (China)—Description and travel. 2. Reynolds, Jim, 1962-
—Journeys—China—Tibet. 3. Priests, Buddhist—Journeys—
China—Tibet.   I. Hallam, Kathleen, 1956-   . II. Title.
DS786.R48   1992
915.1'50458—dc20
    [B]   91-21086
                                                              CIP

The paper used in this publication meets the minimum requirements
of American National Standard for Information Services—Permanence
of Paper for Printed Library Materials, ANSI Z39.48-1084. ∞

Dedication

In memory of Katagiri Roshi, 1928-1990

*"Wherever you go, uphold
the banner of Buddhism."*

Acknowledgements

This journal has come a long way from its original handwritten pages. My thanks to Molly Edgar for patiently deciphering my scribbled notes, Kathleen Hallam for helping to turn them into a cohesive manuscript, Elaine de Man for final copy editing, Susan Cronin-Paris for the book design and cover, and to proofreaders John and Beth Stearns and Sheri Moody. This project would never have been completed without the persistence and dedication of Carol O'Hare.

Thanks to my traveling companions Debbie, Monika, Per, and Pascal for their patient endurance.

This is also an opportunity to tell my family and friends how much I appreciate their support of my explorations of both the outer and inner paths.

Please Note

Distances are given in miles and are only approximate.

As for place names, there are many variations in the transliteration of Tibetan words, so the names used in this book may be different from what is seen elsewhere.

Chinese words appear in *pinyin* form.

CONTENTS

FOREWORD

by His Holiness the Dalai Lama

In his book, *The Outer Path*, Jim Reynolds tells of his travels in Tibet in 1987. Entering Tibet from China, he walked, cycled and sometimes rode on trucks to Lhasa. From there he decided to make the traditional pilgrimage to Mt. Kailas in the western part of the country and subsequently left via Nepal. Despite the misfortunes that have befallen Tibet over the last four decades, he found that the Tibetan people still display the characteristic humor and fortitude for which they have become renowned.

Although the author has a long-standing interest in the practice of Buddhism, his journey in Tibet took on more of the character of a physical challenge and adventure. The rigors of the harsh environment, its vast empty spaces, the extremities of the climate, the altitude and the frequent lack of even the most elementary comfort are enough to test the physical and mental resources of any traveller. That the Tibetans have evolved a contented way of life under such conditions is both a source and an indication of their remarkable resilience in the face of hardship. Due to this, neither the Tibetans in Tibet nor those in exile have lost any of their determination to maintain their identity or regain their freedom.

Whatever difficulties he encountered, the author found they were compensated for by the breathtaking beauty of the landscape and the warmheartedness of the people he met. I am grateful to him for sharing his experiences with others and look forward to the day when we Tibetans will be able to not only travel freely in our own land once more, but also to invite friends like him to join us.

Tenzin Gyatso

His Holiness
the Fourteenth Dalai Lama

April 30, 1991

INTRODUCTION

I teach only Dukkha and the complete cessation of Dukkha.
The Buddha

One summer when I was in high school, I built a
platform high in the branches of a tree in the woods near
my home, and on that platform I painted a big eye. I
envisioned myself up in the tree, meditating, commun-
ing with nature, hardly needing to eat or sleep, and
circling in on the bliss of enlightenment. But I did none
of that. Instead, I played the drums and wiled away the long
summer days in the company of a certain young
woman. The platform with its great eye gazing toward
the stars became a symbol of unfinished business for me.

Years later, in March of 1987, I left my California
home and went to study at a monastery in central
Thailand. For three months I practiced a Burmese form
of Buddhist meditation that cultivates mental awareness.
For as many as fourteen hours a day I focused on being
mindful of every sensation, every thought, every feeling,
and when my time at the monastery came to an end, I
was very close to devoting my life to Buddhism. But I
was still filled with a restless energy, so I decided to re-
enter the world of distractions to see whether my mind
was any more calm, any less troubled by the defilements
of anger, greed and delusion, than it was before I had
gone to Thailand.

I had long been inspired by Tibet and now its pull was stronger than ever. I wanted to explore Himalayan reaches long forbidden to Western eyes and to see areas nearly untouched by Western influence. I wanted to climb through its high mountains, breathe its thin air, endure its fierce weather, and meet its rugged people. I wanted to face every obstacle and overcome every hardship, as I had learned to do in the monastery. But now I would travel the outer path.

I was ready for *dukkha* travel.

I was ready for Tibet.

Arise. Watch. Walk on the right path.
He who follows the right path has joy in this
world and in the world beyond.

Dhammapada, verse 168

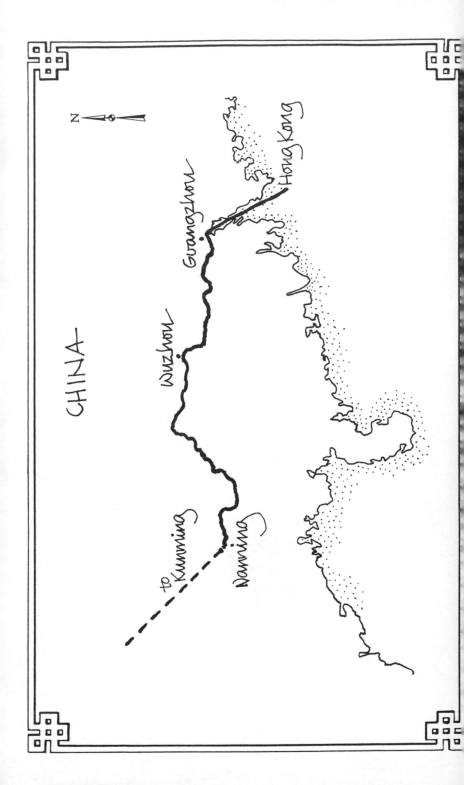

1

CHINA

The Great Way is not difficult for those who have no preferences.
Sengtsan, Hsin Hsin Ming

July 3, 1987 On the ferry to Guangzhou

It is night, and as I cruise out of Hong Kong harbor, the city has never looked better. Seeing the bright skyline against the dark hills, I can forgive Hong Kong for its polluted, tense, money-grubbing atmosphere. I can forgive anything tonight. I'm finally on my way to Tibet.

The noise and the crowds of Hong Kong made me all the more determined to get to Tibet by the less traveled route. Most people go via Kathmandu in Nepal, but my plan is to bicycle from China's Yunnan Province, across eastern Tibet to Lhasa, the capital city. Because this route will take me through territory closed to foreigners, I'll disguise myself as a local on a Chinese bike with my pack tied onto a board over the back wheel.

During my first few days in Hong Kong, I almost gave up on this plan. Everyone I talked to was either skeptical or downright discouraging. Most people told me I was foolish to even try it. Then I met a German couple who had just completed the same trip but in the opposite direction—that is, going down from the high elevations of Tibet to the lower ones of China. They had ridden single-gear bicycles and had had no problems with the authorities. This was exactly what I wanted to hear.

So in the end, my eight days in Hong Kong weren't wasted. I got a three-month visa to travel in China, a $20 bivy sack, a $22 sleeping bag, and a couple of warm jackets.

Now I have a leisurely four-day riverboat ride ahead of me, up the Xijiang River to Nanning.

Goodbye, Hong Kong. I'm off to Tibet.

July 4 Guangzhou

I'm in China. The pleasure it's giving me has caught me by surprise. I got off the ferry at Guangzhou, which used to be known as Canton, and I've been riding around all day on a rented bike—quite an experience. The roads are jammed with cars, buses, pedestrians, horse-drawn carriages, and countless bicycles, all of them black, heavy, single-speed clunkers. To a Westerner, it's unbelievably confusing, but the Chinese bicyclists seem to know what they're doing. I watched one guy maneuver his bike between two cars, tear past a horse, narrowly miss a crowd of pedestrians, and zoom through an intersection just ahead of a roaring bus. There's only one traffic rule: if you can do it without hitting anything, or getting hit, then it's legal. I finally got into it and rang my little bell constantly to clear a path through the chaos.

July 6 On the river to Nanning

From Guangzhou the boat continued on to Wuzhou, and I made some new Chinese friends. I drank plum wine with an enthusiastic old man. *"Gan bei!"* ("Bottoms up!") He was well-educated and spoke English and helped me buy my tickets, translated for me, and gave me advice about how to make a good impression on his countrymen. "Be polite," he said, "and respect local customs." A young student showed me one of his English lessons, a collection of proverbs. The first one was "No pain, no gain"! Another couple, Mr. and Mrs. Chong, have invited me to their home and have offered to show me Nanning. It's hard to imagine that these friendly people are from the same country whose army invaded Tibet in 1950.

China is not at all what I expected. Everyone here wears Western clothes, the crew plays rock music on the boat's loudspeaker, and the people, at least the ones on the boat, seem no worse off economically than other Southeast Asians.

I spend most of my time lying on a wooden bunk watching the scenery go by. And what scenery! As the sun set last night, we passed through a landscape like an old Chinese painting—the mist-shrouded mountains rose straight up over the rice fields along the banks of the river. There is a distinctly different feeling in the air—as if we are going back in time. We steam past small, weather-worn houseboats creeping upriver and water buffalo grazing on the banks. Naked children jump in the water and try to swim up to our boat. But there are also many signs of modernization: tractors, factories, and electric cables strung across the river from huge steel towers.

I've been learning Chinese as fast as I can. The other Westerners got off at Wuzhou, so I shall soon be put to the test.

July 8 Nanning

I'm staying at Mr. and Mrs. Chong's home, a small but comfortable apartment in a high-rise building. The Chongs are generous and helpful and want me to stay here at least four more days to properly see Nanning. I'm anxious to get on to Yunnan, but I also need to watch my tendency to cling to a schedule. If I am not open to the unexpected on this trip, I may miss out on the best things it has to offer.

Anyway, the train to Kunming, my next stop, is not running because there was a flood that washed out the tracks. It would take four grueling days on the bus, and the plane is completely booked. No need to rush. I have only one deadline and that is to meet my friend Doug, who's coming from California, in Lhasa on the first of September. From there, we plan to bicycle together the 600 miles to Kathmandu.

Meanwhile, I'm getting a good picture of Chinese life and culture. The Chongs have a doorbell that plays "Camptown Races" every time someone comes to call. They also keep half a dozen hens on their balcony. They were thrilled when I agreed to exchange $200 cash for their Chinese money. They need the hard currency to buy a bigger TV.

In the Chong's apartment in Nanning with their son

Dinner last night was a leisurely affair with several dishes of meat and vegetables. I've completely gone off my vegetarian diet. Telling the Chinese I don't eat meat is like saying I don't drink water.

I went to the market today and saw some strange and grotesque sights: a bicycle with slabs of raw, unwrapped meat hanging from the rack on the back, a woman walking with a big fish flopping up and down in her small basket, live dogs for sale with their legs chopped off so they couldn't run away.

I also went to the station to check on the train, and everybody there was pushing, shoving, rushing in all directions, and shouting, the usual medium of communication in China. When I finally managed to reach an information window, two Chinese stuck their heads in from the sides, another sneaked in under my arm, and all three yelled their questions before I could get an answer to mine.

Although most people are friendly, those involved with anything official are cold and inflexible.

July 11   Dali

It was with some regret that I left the Chongs, but it was time to move on. I managed to get a seat on a plane to Kunming after all, and from there I got a bus for the 200-mile trip to Dali, where I'm now staying.

This is really is a little piece of paradise. It is nestled between Erhai Lake and the Cangshan Mountain Range. The area is inhabited by the Bai people, one of the many minority groups in China. They cling to their old customs and beliefs, which were severely attacked during the Cultural Revolution of the 1960's. To foreigners, at least, they are very friendly. The women are quite beautiful and wear colorful clothes and voluptuous hairpieces—a welcome relief from the dull green or blue pants and shirts worn by most Chinese in the countryside.

Yesterday I rented a bike and began a 56-mile trip around the lake. I've been trying to get in shape for Tibet, but the toughness of the local people puts me to shame. Even the old women can carry enormous loads on their backs and pull heavily loaded carts up steep mountain roads.

I was making pretty good time, but somewhere on the other side I took a wrong turn and went far into the hills where I passed through some fascinating little towns. The people all stared and laughed at me. I guess they got a kick out of seeing the big foreigner in bright, baggy clothes cruising by on a Chinese bike. After about eight hours, I realized I was quite lost and stopped at a small town to spend the night. The room and outhouse facilities cost 40 cents! The next morning I took a bus to Xiaguan and bicycled back to Dali from there.

July 15 Lijiang

I reached Lijiang by bus; it's about 125 miles from Dali. It has only been open to outsiders for a year and is the last town on the Yunnan-Tibet road where foreigners are permitted. I'll start cycling from here. I've heard that the Chinese are becoming quite sensitive about the freedom bicycles give foreign travelers, and now, if they catch you in closed areas, they not only fine you, but they confiscate the bike as well. I was getting a little apprehensive about run-ins with the police, but I met a Swiss traveler who had just returned from Lhasa and didn't think I'd have too much trouble. He had been able to enter some towns to eat and sleep. So maybe I won't have to travel at night.

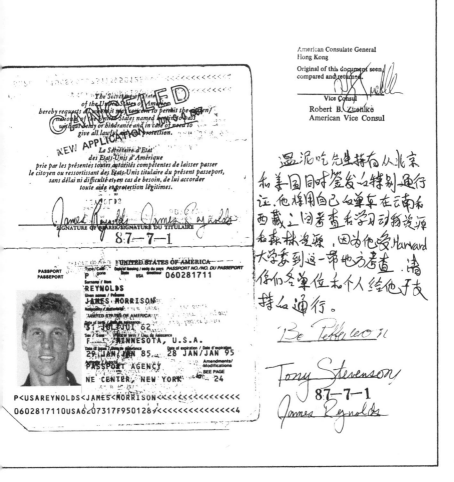

This is the phony document I created using a photocopy of my old passport. It states in Chinese that I have official permission to study the plant and animal life of Yunnan Province and eastern Tibet.

I've also been working on my disguise. I now have a shapeless Mao jacket and a wide-brimmed hat to hide my face and blond hair. And, in case I do get stopped, I have created an impressive-looking document stating that I have official permission to study the area's environment. I started with a photocopy of my old passport that the U.S. embassy in Hong Kong gave me when they issued me a new passport. (The old one mistakenly identified me as female.) The paper is stamped with the U.S. government seal and looks very official. I had a Chinese restaurant owner I met in Dali write on it in Chinese that I work for Harvard and have permission from Beijing and Washington to study the plant and animal life of Yunnan Province and eastern Tibet. I stapled my photo onto it and put signatures all over the page. Then I went to the market-place to get a rubber stamp for the date (87-7-1) and had to buy a separate stamp for each individual number, plus a little one for the hyphen. The document looks important, but I don't know who it's going to fool.

July 16

I did a lot of running around today. I bought my bike and some make-shift gear and went with a few other Westerners to visit Dr. Wu, an herbalist in a nearby village. But tonight I don't feel much inclination to describe the scene. I'm beginning to wonder if this is all just a foolish waste of time. I am driven by restlessness and my desire to devour more and more of the world. I run here, I run there, but go nowhere. Every day my body is in a different place, but I don't know if my mind and my heart have traveled as well. My journal is growing, but am I?

Dr. Wu, herbalist

July 17

I spent another day shopping for gear and bought a pair of large, bamboo baskets to hang over the back wheel and hold all my belongings. I'm really rather proud of my bicycle. It's a typical sturdy Chinese bike with one-speed, fat tires, and good brakes. Not bad for $40.

I plan to leave tomorrow morning. Getting ready for the trip has been a little nerve-wracking, and I'm hoping the bicycling will relax me.

Right now the idea of a solitary journey appeals to me. I'm still trying to preserve a bit of the mindfulness and concentration I worked so hard to develop at the Buddhist meditation center in Thailand. I left only a month ago, but it already seems in the distant past. Sometimes I think my three months there were wasted. I may be on the verge of becoming a monk, but I'm not sure I accomplished anything more meditating there than the realization that I was trying too hard, that I was attempting to find a short-cut to enlightenment. In one sense, hitting the road as a traveler is the opposite extreme of sitting immobile in a monastery

Disguised as a Chinese bicyclist

hut, yet I feel a sense of continuity. In stillness or in movement, I wander on, gradually finding my way. At least traveling alone, there will be more opportunity to watch my thoughts, to be quiet and relatively serene.

July 18 Taking a breather by the side of the road

I left Lijiang this morning at 7:00 and rode 30 miles to Baihanchang—20 miles of muscle-training uphill followed by 10 miles of long, wild downhill. I ate lunch as inconspicuously as possible at a roadside restaurant and then joined the main road heading north. I continued down through a beautiful valley patchworked with corn and other vegetables, dotted with little brown cottages, and surrounded by rolling green hills. Groups of children yelled "hellooo," and beautiful girls gave me big smiles.

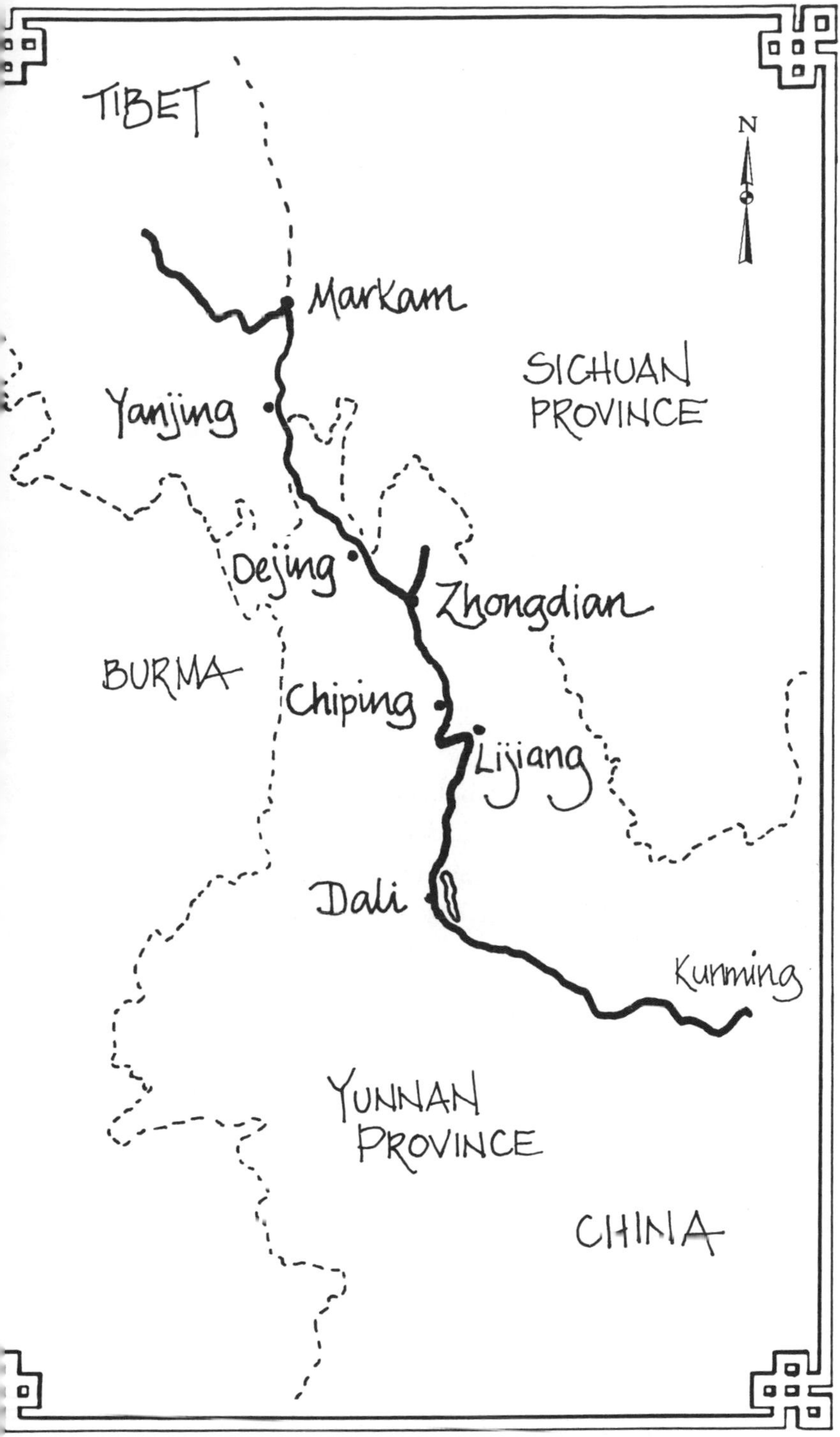

TIBET
N
Markam
SICHUAN
PROVINCE
Yanjing
Dejing
Zhongdian
BURMA
Chiping
Lijiang
Dali
Kunming
YUNNAN
PROVINCE
CHINA

I was just visited by a curious old man. His big grin was nearly toothless as he offered me some *jiu*, a potent clear Chinese alcohol. He also showed me his handsome jade and silver jewelry, which is apparently very old. He didn't want to sell it. He was just very proud to show it to me.

My disguise seems to work pretty well even though I'm a foot taller than most Chinese. When I'm riding the bike, you can't tell I'm a Westerner until I'm about 15 feet away. From the back you can't tell at all. When I get close, people look very surprised to see I'm not Chinese.

From where I sit now, I can see more severe mountains looming ahead.

Evening Chiping

I've been invited into the home of a family in Chiping, a small village set on a hillside overlooking a river, about 44 miles from Lijiang. A young man, about my age, saw me on the road and invited me to his home for a meal. I still had plenty of energy left for cycling, but a dinner invitation was hard to turn down.

The entire house is like a museum piece from the middle ages. The courtyard has a warm, homey feel to it. Hens and roosters run around the open space, scratching and pecking, and often have to be chased out of the bedrooms by the mother. The wooden walls are decoratively carved and covered with lattice. There is a separate room for drying meat which is rather eerie. It is dark and dusty, and legs, heads and various other animal parts hang from the ceiling. In the kitchen corn flour is stored in large, flat wicker containers.

Children of Chiping

Shortly after I arrived the young man's father brought out the *jiu*, and soon I was too drunk to continue cycling. Luckily they asked me to spend the night. Dinner was delicious. The main dish was a combination of stir-fried eggs, peppers, and pork. We also had pan-fried breads and vegetables. No rice!

After dinner I took a walk down to the river and was stirred by the lushness of the cultivated crops and the green mountains. Soon, however, the children discovered me, and I was pounced on by a horde of curious kids. I joked and played tag with them. They laughed and stared at me. And word by word they taught me some more Chinese.

Now we've gotten into some serious late night drinking. The father and I trade shots and cheer each other on. One of his friends has joined us, as well as many of the villagers. The room is packed with people who've come to see what strange things the foreigner will do, and I'm having a hard time finding the balance between keeping them entertained and not making a complete ass of myself.

As I write, the father and his friend appear to be in a political argument. Although I can only catch bits of the conversation, the words "Mao Zedong", "Deng Xiaoping" and *"qian"* (money) come up often.

Watch out! The argument between the father and his friend is getting heated, and they're nearly at blows. Other people have now stepped in between them and joined in the argument. It's quite a party.

July 19

I feel wretched—very weak and suffering from bad diarrhea. In the middle of the night I felt my bowels clench, but I didn't know where the toilet was. I rushed out of the bedroom, knowing I only had a few moments to spare, and frantically searched for the outhouse. I didn't have time to find my flashlight, so I groped my way towards the nearest bush. But before I got my pants down, my self-control completely gave out and my bowels exercised their relief in my shorts. I swear this is one of the most humiliating experiences a person can have. You can't imagine what the word "emergency" means until you experience the exploding diarrhea of Asia. Even more embarrassing was trying to explain to the mother with gestures why I needed to borrow her washbasin and soap.

The karmic law of cause and effect is not so mysterious: I drink, I get hungover. There is no way I can bike today.

Later

This evening I felt a little better and the father took me down to the main street in town where a big celebration was going on. The children were all carrying torches and singing. Then the father began to yell *"Wo bao che"* and march through the streets. Soon all the children joined us in a parade of firelit smiles and continuous calls of *"Wo bao che."* I don't know the exact translation of *"Wo bao che,"* but I think it was a Chinese version of "Paaartee!" That was all I needed to know, and soon I joined in the chorus myself. I felt as if I was in some mysterious dream of another world. Faces faded in and out of the night. Everyone was happy. Everything seemed right.

July 20

I'm beginning to get some of my strength back and the call of the diarrhea is less urgent. However, it's been raining all morning, and, again, I'm prevented from continuing on my way. I would like to be in Tibet at least by my 25th birthday, on July 31.

Evening   Small town past Zhongdian

I left Chiping this afternoon, accepting a ride on an old green army truck. We soon left the lush river valley and went up, up, up through spectacular gorges with rushing streams and then further and further up through thick forests of huge pines. The mountains were as steep and as rugged as I've ever seen.

After about 50 miles, the driver dropped me off and I got back on my bike, but I soon felt the effect of the altitude. Lijiang was about 8000 feet, and it's much higher here. I was struggling uphill, short of breath, light-headed, and a little nauseous, when another Chinese truck with two drivers stopped and offered me a lift the remaining 30 miles to Zhongdian. They were both friendly and helpful and refused to accept money for the ride. They didn't seem to care that I wasn't supposed to be there.

One form of transportation: a Chinese army truck

Zhongdian is a renowned trouble spot for foreigners, and I left as quickly and inconspicuously as possible. The place reminded me of a frontier town. The people seemed tough, dirty, even a little threatening—until I said "hello." Then they opened up with big, broad smiles.

I was soon in the countryside again, and after a few miles, the road leveled off onto a beautiful, open, cultivated plateau dotted with small groups of houses. The culture is becoming less Chinese and more Tibetan with each passing mile. I'm getting into a section of Yunnan Province that was actually part of Tibet before the Chinese invaded and redrew the boundaries.

Even the people here look radically different. Gone are the short Chinese in their drab clothing. Here, big burly men wear corduroy coats, fur vests, or heavy woolen overcoats. They look like rugged Western cowboys with dark tans. The women wear brightly colored aprons and beautiful jewelry.

I'm happy to be getting into more Tibetan territory. Tonight, for the first time, I saw prayer flags on the tops of houses. Tibetans print Buddhist mantras or prayers to various deities on these colored flags. Every gust of wind blows the prayers across the land, earning merit for their owners.

At dusk I came to a group of large, high, white-walled houses and began to ask people by the road if there was a place I could sleep or buy food. I knew there were no restaurants, but I hoped to buy some food from the locals. After a short time I came upon a muscular man who looked me over, then smiled broadly and invited me into his house. His wife and kids were excited to have a foreign guest, and soon we were all having a great time.

My host's youngest son gave me my first Tibetan language lesson. I also had my first taste of *tsampa*, the Tibetan staple made from roasted barley flour and tea and eaten uncooked. You're supposed to knead it together into a doughy ball, but I made a real mess and got flour all over the floor. It should do a good job of clogging up my intestines. We had some delicious goat's milk yogurt and thick butter tea, which is a mixture of black tea, salt, and rancid yak butter. I liked it.

The father, Tsarong, kept looking at a picture of His Holiness the Dalai Lama in my Lonely Planet guidebook. The Dalai Lama is the spiritual and political leader of Tibetans and is considered a "god-king" by his people, an incarnation of Avalokiteshvara, the Buddha of Compassion.

The present Dalai Lama escaped to India in 1959, after the Chinese crushed a Tibetan revolt. Since then, the Chinese have forbidden the Tibetans to have any pictures of him, so I had brought photocopies with me to give away. Tsarong seemed pleased when I offered him one.

He took the photo, wrapped it in a white cloth, and placed it face down on the little altar—above which hangs a big poster of Mao. Elsewhere in China, the Mao posters were taken down long ago, but I suspect the reforms of the post-Cultural Revolution era have not yet arrived here, and Tsarong probably still fears persecution.

Since I can't speak Tibetan, I have to be creative to communicate with my hosts. I showed them pictures of my family. They loved the trim clothes and hairstyles of my American parents, but I don't think they knew what to make of the pictures of me and my old blues band. I'm sure they've never seen a drum set or an electric guitar before.

Tsarong was also very interested in my camera, which I had purchased, used, for 50 cents at the Goodwill store back in California. When I indicated that I wanted to take a picture of them, the oldest boy rushed to put on his "cool" Western-style jacket, and the mother took off many of her colorful work clothes.

The first Tibetan family I stayed with

Tsarong and his family live in a two-story house built around a courtyard. The first floor is a stable, a mess of mud, straw and dung. It is filled with bulls, pigs, piglets, chickens, and cows that look like yaks. There is also a big, black, furry mastiff on a massive chain, which is a major inconvenience. I still have diarrhea despite huge doses of Kaopectate, and every time I go outside to use the toilet, which is just an open, muddy trench next to the house, Tsarong has to restrain the dog.

The people live on the second floor, where the high ceilings are supported by wooden pillars two-feet in diameter. There are decoratively carved cupboards along the walls and big, square-edged doorjambs and ceiling beams. I saw lots of wooden plank barrels around—like something the pilgrims at Plymouth would have used—and many fur, woven-hair, and woolen clothes and blankets.

In the middle of the largest room there is a huge iron cauldron made up of four separate pots of different sizes welded together. There is a large fire constantly burning beneath it, and a hole in the roof above it lets out the smoke. Directly above the hearth a soot-covered, lattice shelf hangs from the ceiling where meat is being smoked. The floor is made of unevenly laid planks, so some of the sounds and smells from the stable below filter up. Tonight I will be lulled to sleep by grunts and clucks, accompanied by the potent, but not unpleasant, odor of fresh manure.

July 21 Penzola

After a big breakfast of *tsampa*, yogurt, and cheese, I said my good-byes and rode off. It wasn't long before I was offered a ride by a pair of Chinese truck drivers who were heading to Litang. I was glad for the lift as I was still feeling sick and weak. We made good time through sparsely populated areas until we were stopped by a series of mudslides in a broad valley. Fifty women workers, using only hand hoes, were slowly clearing the huge pile of mud from the road. They all stopped, stared, and smiled when they saw me. I said "hello," and they giggled and answered "heelloo."

On the other side of the valley, we could see a small Tibetan village where a procession of Buddhist monks in their brownish-red robes wove their way single file around the houses. I could hear them chanting as they walked up and down the switchbacks of the steep slope. The young Chinese truck drivers didn't know what the monks were doing and didn't seem to care.

Ever since the invasion, the Chinese have attempted to eradicate the practice of Buddhism in Tibet. They destroyed thousands of monasteries and monuments and imprisoned monks or sent them to labor camps. They made it illegal to study the teachings of the Buddha and burned libraries full of Buddhist scriptures. In recent years, the Chinese have supposedly relaxed these policies for propaganda purposes, but I still wonder to what extent religious expression is actually tolerated.

Tibetan Buddhism with its exotic, mystical rituals is quite different from the forms of Buddhism I've practiced. Tibetan monks engage in deep, other-worldly polyphonic chanting in dark, lamp-lit monasteries; devoted meditators live in icy caves on psychic heat alone; and enlightened beings are embued with supernatural powers. I have great respect for these monks, but I have never been drawn to the esoteric Tibetan practices. I am inclined more toward the simple "clean the toilet and be mindful" approach of

Zen, of being aware of the present moment. The nuts and bolts approach of developing the mind in Theravada, the form of Buddhism I studied in Thailand, also appeals to me.

Eventually the truck got through the slide area and rolled on for another hour. The drivers, who were going on to Litang, let me off at a fork in the road by the swollen, fast-flowing Jinsha River. There three uniformed men armed with machine guns stood guard at the bridge. Feigning confidence, I began to push my bike across the bridge. One of the guards stepped forward and loudly asked where I was going.

"Lhasa," I said.

He shrugged his shoulders and said, "Okay."

I said, "Goodbye," and got back on my bike and rode quickly away.

I struggled on to a good-sized village where it began to rain, so I decided to get a bed in the hotel.

Now I am very tired and have little energy. I'm not sure if it is the altitude, the strain of bicycling, or some nasty virus. I'm trying to keep my spirits up, but sick and alone, out in the Asian countryside, I really feel the weight of human solitude.

July 22

It rained all day today. I felt weak and slept most of the morning. When I walked into the restaurant for lunch, I was surprised to see two Swiss women sitting there, waiting for a bus to Dejing. Their names were Debbie and Monika and they, too, were on their way to Lhasa. Foreigners, of course, aren't allowed on buses, but they told me they just bought their tickets and no one said anything.

We talked a few minutes, until their bus was ready to leave. Then we wished each other good luck.

Now I'm depressed and worried about my physical condition. Will my body hold out to fulfill the plans I have for it? Sickness is *dukkha*!

I'm trying to use this experience as an opportunity to contemplate Dhamma, the teachings of the Buddha. I know that it is my attachment to things, people, even my "self," that is the cause of my discontent. And I know that such attachments are the cause of all the world's troubles, of *dukkha*. I understand that *dukkha* is all the sufferings of life: dissatisfaction, separation from loved ones, pain, illness, old age, and death.

I know all these things, but right now I'd rather be biking.

July 23 On the way to Dejing

The rain finally stopped and my strength returned, so I got an early start on the bike today. Even so, I made less than 20 miles. The road rises, rises, rises toward the pass before Dejing, and I saw my first snow-capped Himalayan mountain. The landscape is beginning to overwhelm me. Everything is mammoth. And the altitude makes even normal movement difficult.

The area is thickly forested but heavily logged. I've heard the Chinese have clear-cut large areas of eastern Tibet and shipped the lumber to China.

About 4:00 this afternoon I passed two local Tibetan men lounging in the sun in front of what looked like an abandoned motel or old logging barracks. They convinced me to stay the night. The pass, they said, was still another 30 kilometers (18 miles) away.

Two Tibetan friends

The three of us had a great time. They fed me rice, fried greens, and boiled meat. They just spit the bones on the floor and let the dogs clean up the mess. It took us a while to explain our jokes and stories using only panto-mimes and simple Chinese. They sang songs from their village, and one did an impressive, high-stepping local dance. I danced rock'n'roll style, and they fell on the floor laughing. Then I sang a few American folk and rock songs. They especially liked Janice Joplin's "Mercedes Benz."

July 24

My progress without trucks is pretty slow. I keep wondering if I'll make it to Markam, a Tibetan town just past the border, before my birthday, only a week away. Then I have to remind myself, "Present moment, Jim. Live in the present moment."

The culture is becoming very Tibetan. The local men, with their long hair, high cheekbones, long noses, and dark skin look like American Indians. Everyone seems to speak both Chinese and Tibetan, and all the people I pass on the road wear Tibetan dress. I even saw a monastery being constructed. Six thousand Buddhist monasteries were destroyed by the Red Guard during the Cultural Revolution, but it was impossible for the Chinese to destroy the faith of these people. Buddhism is inextricable from Tibetan culture, as essential as air. Since 1980, however, the Chinese have tried to undo some of the damage by allowing a number of monasteries to be rebuilt.

Later Dejing

I've been nabbed by the police!

This morning I was offered a ride by a Chinese truck driver who said he was going to Markam. I thought I was very fortunate to find a ride going so far, but when we pulled into Dejing the driver told me to get my bike down, and a Chinese policeman appeared instantly. It felt like a set up, and I wondered if the driver would receive a reward for turning in an illegal foreigner. He disappeared, and I was left to deal with the *Gong An*, as the Chinese police are called. I wasn't sure what would happen. It was quite possible I'd be fined or have my bike confiscated. It was almost certain they would force me to go back. I tried to act confident as I was led to the police station.

The officers read to me from their police manual in the best English they could muster: "You are in an area closed to foreigners," they said. "You must return."

I showed them my passport and phony document and tried to look sincere while I insisted I had official permission to be there. The document did look impressive. Unfortunately it lacked the one thing they were looking for—the official Chinese red stamp.

They got me a room at the government hotel, and here I wait for their pronouncement.

July 25

Yesterday afternoon the *Gong An* informed me I would have to return the way I came. They were courteous and never mentioned fining me. They also told me that two Swiss women had been caught as well and that the three of us would be sent on a bus back to Zhongdian today.

The police kept my passport, so I was free to roam the town, since I couldn't leave without it. I found Debbie and Monika right away, and the three of us drank local beer in the restaurant and lamented our bad luck. It was great to speak English again and trade stories about our experiences getting here. They are as determined as I am to reach Lhasa by this route, and we vowed we wouldn't give up.

July 26 Outside of Zhongdian

The Dejing police were polite but firm this morning, as they put the three of us on a bus out of town, dutifully making us promise we would return to the area open to foreigners. In reality we were plotting ways to escape and try again.

The *Gong An* bought our tickets, though, of course, we had to pay for them. They escorted us to the bus and secured my bicycle on top. Later we discovered that one of them was sitting a few seats away from us. When the bus stopped at the logging barracks, I jumped off to say hello to my friends there. The officer hurried after me to make sure I didn't run for it.

As we retraced the route I had worked so hard to get through this past week, and I saw the sights and scenery for a second time, I began to rethink my bicycle plan. Considering my intermittent bouts of illness, it would be better to try to hitchhike with Debbie and Monika.

Luckily I was able to sell my bike to one of the passengers on the bus. He was a Khampa, one of the native people of the Kham region of eastern Tibet. He wore a long, black robe tied with a wide, cloth belt and carried a two-foot sword and a big wad of money. I sold him the bike for $20, half of what I paid for it, and gave him most of my tools and my pump.

The bus reached Zhongdian by late afternoon, and we expected to be met by the local police who would escort us back to Lijiang, the town where foreigners are permitted. But no one was waiting for us, and our escort from Dejing simply got off and walked away. Debbie, Monika, and I slipped off the bus as quickly and as inconspicuously as possible, but just before we rounded the corner the Khampa who had bought my bike yelled, "Hey, this thing has a flat!" It must have gone flat on top of the bus, but I wasn't about to stop now. Glancing at his long knife, we hastened our retreat.

We decided to try the other road out of Zhongdian, the one leading 265 miles up to Litang in Sichuan Province. We took side streets and back alleys through town to avoid the police. But as we turned one corner, we found ourselves right in front of the police station where half a dozen policemen stood staring at us. Amazingly they said nothing. So we pretended we belonged there and walked right past them.

Another form of transportation: a road maintenance tractor

Once we got out of town, we hiked through the countryside until we were offered a ride a short distance in the back of a long, low road maintenance tractor. Later, as evening approached, we came upon a man and his teenage daughter who were camped by the side of the road with their two yaks. We asked if we could share their cooking fire, and they invited us to stay the night in their tent, which was simply a large, white tarp pitched by the side of the road. The girl was a master at manipulating the fire for cooking, adding just enough yak dung to get the right amount of heat. For us, it was camping, but for them, it was everyday life.

I think our luck has changed. I get along well with Debbie and Monika, and we are feeling the joy of again being free and on our own

July 27

Today, after going 20 miles, we found out that the road to Litang was washed out. Now we have to return to

Zhongdian to try the Dejing route a second time and are waiting at a logging camp for a ride back to town. I hate backtracking. For the last two days my mind has been filled with <u>ifs</u>. If I had gone from Kathmandu or taken the legal way through northern China, I would have been in Tibet a month already. If I had stayed on an earlier truck going to Litang instead of getting off at the bridge, I would have been past Markam five days ago. But here I am. No use complaining. Just deal with it.

July 30

The last few days have been hard traveling, but I finally made it past Dejing again. The day we spent at the lumber camp waiting for a truck was real torture. We waited there for ten hours and, even then, only Monika was able to get a ride. People would tell us different places to go to get rides, but all of them were wrong. The few drivers we actually talked to were simply rude.

Chinese drivers are generally equatable with *dukkha*. A common attitude among the Chinese is that foreigners are decadent devils, to be treated accordingly. The difference between them and the warm, open, playful Tibetans is striking. The Tibetans are also infinitely more generous. The one bright spot in the day was when I traded my mountaineering glasses for a hand-made fur vest.

By nightfall Debbie and I were still sitting in the rain, pissed off and muttering that favorite phrase of independent Western travelers in China, "fucking Chinese." Finally a few of the local people began to have pity on us. They brought us warm rice and vegetables, and we sat in the middle of the road in the pouring rain devouring this feast. Then the same kind souls found us a place to sleep,

gave us tea and warm water for washing, and lined up a
ride for us in the morning. We were able to get a good
night's sleep after all.

When we caught up to Monika the next day in
Zhongdian, we felt lucky for our night of luxury. She had
waited for us on the outskirts of town until midnight and
then slept fitfully in the rain, wrapped in her poncho,
harassed all night by a huge, growling dog.

Reunited, we set off for Dejing—for the second time.
We went about 20 miles, then stopped for the night at a
small town where we found a tiny clothing store crammed
with garments hanging everywhere. We decided to
disguise ourselves in local attire, and the people in the
shop had a good laugh trying to teach me how to properly
tie my *chuba*, the black corduroy robe Tibetans wear.

*Disguised as a Tibetan with
my chuba tied around my waist*

That night we spent a pleasant evening around a campfire outside of town, eating peanuts and drinking beer. I sang Bob Dylan songs while Monika and Debbie tried to sew some Tibetan-looking clothes to augment their disguise. A truck driver who pulled in late that night promised to take us to Dejing if we met him at his truck at 7:00 the next morning. The alarm clock failed to go off, however, and we didn't wake up until 7:20. A golden opportunity had passed, and now we had to wait by the side of the road again. Would we ever get to Tibet?

Finally a truck stopped, but it could take only one passenger. Since Debbie and Monika wanted to stay together, I grabbed it. My two friends are as determined as I am to take this route to Lhasa, so they understood. We will meet again, I'm sure.

After several truck rides, I arrived outside of dreaded Dejing at 6:00 in the evening. I had the driver drop me off near some woods about five miles from town. He charged me six *yuan*, about $1.20, an outrageous amount by local standards. It was the first time I've had to pay for a ride.

My plan was to hide until dark, then cross the valley to the Yanjing road, and completely bypass Dejing. It was relaxing to sit alone in the quiet woods—until it began to rain. I set off down the valley, crossed the swollen stream, but soon lost the path as darkness and thick fog set in.

I decided to bed down for the night but was unable to find a level spot on the slippery, steep slope. Everything I had on was soaking wet. I crawled inside my tent without setting it up, pulled a tarp over me, and propped up my umbrella. It was a long, sleepless night. I was still wearing all my wet clothes, and shivered as the night got colder. I was quite happy to see the dawn.

In the morning, I headed uphill toward the road. Because of the altitude, I had to stop every ten or fifteen steps to catch my breath. Three times the police zoomed by on some unknown business, and I managed to dodge them each time. I wondered whether yesterday's driver had informed on me. Later I got a ride on a tractor that took me 16 miles to another logging camp. At the top of a steep hill the driver cut the engine to save gas and coasted full speed down the winding road with no guard rails between us and the valley below. It was like a mad roller coaster ride. You just have to have faith that you'll survive.

Now I'm past Dejing and back in high mountains— cool air, rushing streams, and a few snow-covered peaks.

The police just drove by again. They didn't see me, but that's the fourth time they've come by in their van.

It is beautiful here, but I am too tense to enjoy it. I'm only 125 miles—one good truck ride—from Markam. I've heard that once you get past that town, there is little chance of being caught by the police. If they send me back again, I don't know what I'll do.

July 31

It's my 25th birthday today, but that doesn't mean very much here.

In trying to avoid the police, it's difficult to know whether it's best to keep moving or stay put. I'd like to meet up with Monika and Debbie again, but I don't know if they are ahead of or behind me. I've also heard that the road ahead is washed out, and it won't be fixed for four days. This eliminates any chance I might have had of getting a ride on a truck coming from Dejing. So this morning I decided to start walking. I can't wait any longer.

Later

I made it past the washout with no trouble and walked another four miles with my feet on fire. My heavy army boots are killing my feet and are more than I need for walking on a dirt road, but last week I stupidly gave away my sneakers to lighten my load.

The road was cut into the side of a steep mountain that plunged into a wild, monsoon-swollen river filled with thick, reddish brown water. Its power was apparent everywhere. In some places it had shoved huge piles of mud out of its path, and in others it had carved and gouged the land.

After awhile I came upon a group of well-kept houses sitting on a cultivated plateau and asked the local people if I could buy food. Eventually I was invited to spend the night.

I get a mixed reaction from people here. They're friendly, but somehow suspicious, reserved, and, at times, rude. The children helped me wash my clothes in the stream, but once they found out I had Dalai Lama pictures, they begged mercilessly for all of them, until I sent them away.

There's a lot I want to write, but I'm pretty tired. I'm glad I'll have a bed tonight.

August 1

I'm feeling queasy. I have diarrhea again, and the blisters on my feet are infected. What next?

This area seems different. From Zhongdian to Dejing people dressed in traditional clothes and were generally very friendly. But on this side of Dejing people are back to wearing Chinese Mao suits and they seem colder.

I'm beginning to feel foolish wearing my disguise. I suppose I present a pretty bizarre picture with my Mao cap, my thick fur vest, and my robe tied around my waist like a skirt. Worse, I haven't shaved for a week, or bathed for two.

Later Shung Sui Village

Although I still felt sick, I set off walking this morning as there was no prospect of getting a ride on a truck. At least I would make some progress.

The day turned out to be an unexpectedly nice one. The clear, blue sky set off the mountains like purple, green and orange jewels. I began to feel better and my feet didn't hurt as much. I even got a ride in a tiny front-loading dump truck packed with people hanging from it in every direction. I tried to take a picture of them, but as soon as I got out my camera, everyone jumped off and wouldn't get back on until I put it away.

A man we passed on the road leading a string of donkeys invited me and some of the others to sit and drink *suyu cha* (butter tea) with him. The mood was serene and reflective, and I didn't feel the need to entertain, to be the goofy foreigner for them.

After an hour or so I hit the road again and soon came to another landslide blocking the road. I had to hide underneath a parked truck with a bunch of beautiful, laughing road crew girls while explosives were used to clear it. Later on, I met a young local man named Korang who spoke English surprisingly well. It was wonderful to hear my language again. He invited me to stay at his home.

Korang lives in a small village perched above the river. It feels good to be here. I'm not worried about the police, so I can relax and enjoy the people and the beauty of the place without feeling the need to rush on.

I found out why people around here aren't wearing the *chuba*. It isn't political after all. It's simply too hot during the summer. Korang has been a great source of information.

August 2 By the side of the road

I started out feeling sick again this morning, but unlike yesterday, I felt worse as the day went on. I walked nine miles before I got to a measly truck stop. Nine miles is not very far, but I was feeling feverish and the river valley was swelteringly hot. Carrying my cold weather clothes is a burden. My big leather boots are hot, heavy, and killing my feet. Again I regretted giving away my sneakers.

I simply couldn't go on, and when I finally found some shade, I stopped and took a nap. I don't know if it's the physical exertion, the altitude, the food and water, or the combination that's making me feel sick. I'm still suffering from queasiness, diarrhea, and general weakness.

The workers say the road from Dejing won't be open for five or six days. Today there was not one vehicle of any sort going my way. If I have to walk the 22 miles to Yanjing, I may die.

I didn't meet anyone interesting today—only a stupid Chinese man who pestered me until I took his picture. Today I really asked myself why I'm doing this. Maybe all this suffering is a karmic answer to my delusions about the thrill of travel. Or maybe it's some kind of metaphor for the difficulties of attaining enlightenment that I'll appreciate later. Much later.

August 3

Would you believe it! Just after I finished writing last night, after I had my tent set up and was finally beginning to relax, a truck full of people came by headed for Yanjing. I frantically packed up and heaved my stuff on board.

The truck is an old, beat up, green dinosaur. Every time we came to a landslide in the road, the Tibetan passengers would begin to chant and pray for this pitiful vehicle. Its gears ground with agony as the driver forced it into low. Then it crawled over the mud, leaning precariously towards the edge of the cliff that drops into the churning river below.

Now I'm sitting at the side of the road, wagering with myself on whether the truck driver will drink twenty-five cups of tea or only twenty. I'm antsy to go and have to keep reminding myself, "Don't just do something. Sit there!"

Can it be that the driver has had enough tea now? He actually seems to be loading up. I may get somewhere before dusk after all.

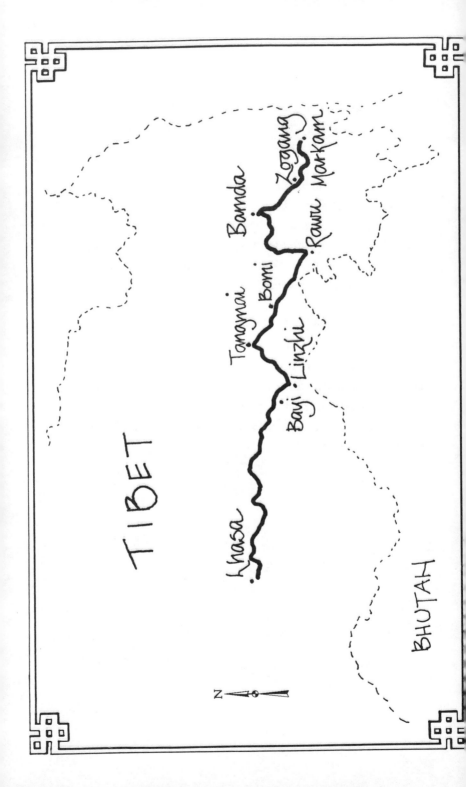

2

EASTERN TIBET

*Nothing is unbearable to those who have made forbearance all
their own and who are great in the correct appreciation of the true
nature of things.*

Jatakamala, Jataka Nidana

August 4 Markam!

I finally reached Markam. I'm now officially in Tibet,
or what the Chinese call the Tibet Autonomous Region of
the People's Republic of China.

The old truck took me 70 miles straight through
Yanjing and over a pass in the mountains to Markam. This
town is supposed to be a trouble spot for illegal travelers,
but so far so good. I've even got a ride lined up for tomorrow.

I've been suffering from what I presume is altitude
sickness. I feel weak and am worried I won't have the
strength for any trekking. I would like to hike into those
beautiful mountains away from the road.

The wide-faced, fierce-looking Khampa men are
everywhere here. They're proud, confident, and usually
good-looking. Their hair is about three feet long, and they
twist it like a rope, tie a bright red tassel to the end, then
wrap all of it around the top of their head like a turban.
They also carry their long knives in ornate sheaths at their
waist. This afternoon I tried to carry on a conversation
with two Khampas outside the hotel. They held fresh
goats' heads in each hand and told me they were tasty. I
tried to take a picture of them, but they would only let me
photograph the heads.

Hanging out with a Khampa dude in Markam

So it is with photos. Most of the really fascinating things I've seen, I'm not able to get shots of. I wish I had gotten a picture of the truck that brought me into town today. There were seventeen bizarre individuals hanging on in back, along with chickens, clanking cookery on strings, and big leather bags of grain.

Main street Markam is dark and dusty and filled with all sorts of shady-looking characters dressed in dirty, ragged layers of clothes. It's a tough place, like the Wild West. Chinese run the restaurants and stores, which are little more than unpainted wooden shacks, while the Khampas, with their rifles slung across their backs, roam the streets and gallop in and out of town on their horses.

Old men gather at outdoor pool tables, and there are lots of toothless or gold-toothed smiles. Strings of mules with colorful blankets, ornate pack saddles, and bridles wander through town. Pigs and chickens run around everywhere.

Little runny-nosed kids are both curious and afraid of me. But I attract attention from more than them when I walk down the street—stares and giggles from the pretty girls and wisecracks from the young Khampa dudes hanging out by the lumber pile. Yet, almost everyone responds with a smile if I give a nod, "hello."

August 5

My ride fell through—the driver refused to take me. Now what?

August 6

Yesterday, late in the evening, I decided to walk up to the crossroads because I was tired of sitting in the hotel alone. I was starved for some sort of conversation beyond hand signals and telling people I was American, and I thought maybe I'd run into some other Westerners. But when I got to the crossroads, I found no one. Then, as I was heading back to my hotel, I saw Debbie and Monika walking toward me! We greeted each other with hugs and went to the restaurant for a huge meal and lots of beer to celebrate being together again. We exchanged stories and compared notes on each little town and road washout along the way. It had taken them three days to get a ride from where I left them. They spent one night in a wood-shed but were chased out at midnight by a group of yelling, sword-waving men. It was very late when we returned to the hotel.

August 7

I thought once we got to Markam everything would be easy, but we just found out that the truck drivers will get fined if they are caught carrying foreigners. That explains why, yesterday, we sat by the side of the road from 9:00 in the morning until 9:00 at night. Many trucks passed, but none would stop for us. That was frustrating enough, but now we are getting the run-around from the Chinese drivers in town. They tell us they're going to leave tomorrow, and then they take off down the road. One driver, who's staying at our hotel, promised he would leave this afternoon at 2:00. When 2:00 rolled around, he said he would leave at 4:00. At 4:00 he said he'd leave tomorrow.

Local people aren't much better. They are always happy to give us information, but it's usually wrong. It's hard to know whether they're ignorant, incompetent, or hostile and laughing behind our backs. Now that I finally made it to Markam, I wonder if I will ever be able to leave.

It rained off and on all day today, and a chill set in. We stayed warm and dry in a roadside restaurant and ate soup and noodles to console ourselves. We played cards outside, under an umbrella, and had to hide in a muddy ditch when a police van drove by.

Sitting in the ditch, Monika and I made up our own blues songs. Buddhism and the blues are both expressions of and responses to *dukkha*. The lyrics came easily. We sang "The lyin' driver blues," "The endless ditch waitin' rain-soaked blues," and of course, "The explodin' hot buns diarrhea blues," all to the tune of Muddy Water's "Mannish Boy."

Sometimes I forget that I am experiencing exactly what I'd hoped to experience. But that's typical for me. Once I have what I want, I want something different. I'm never fully satisfied. Didn't I learn anything meditating in Thailand?

I just wish I didn't have to be worried about the police when I walk up and down the street. And I am sure I would enjoy this town much more if I knew I could leave.

August 9 (I think) Zogang

I'm not sure whether our story is a melodrama or a black comedy.

When we returned to the hotel in Markam two days ago, we found out that none of the truck drivers would take foreigners—even if we offered them a lot of money. We really thought this was the end of the line. In despair we made plans to turn back. But, as usual, when the last bit of hope had vanished, our luck changed.

We met a Chinese truck driver at our hotel who was getting extremely drunk. He said he was leaving for Zogang (100 miles away) at 3:00 in the morning, and he'd take us if we paid twice the normal price. We weren't sure if he was telling the truth, but we got up at 2:30 and by 4:00, amazingly enough, we were driving out of Markam, our pockets a little emptier, and our driver only slightly more sober.

It was the worst drive I've ever experienced. For twelve hours we sat in a cramped space on top of the cargo in back. Most of the time I had stomach pains and diarrhea from the altitude. Zogang is about 14,500 feet above sea level, and the passes we crossed on the way are 2000 feet higher. Fortunately, I felt better as soon as I got out of the truck.

For most of the ride we were completely covered by the canvas tarp. This was partly to protect us from the rain but mostly to hide us as we passed the Chinese checkpoints. I could see through a rip in the tarp and gazed longingly at mountains more amazing and inviting than any I've ever seen: terrifyingly steep valleys, surging streams, thick pine forests, and beautiful, huge rock outcroppings. I was tempted to get out of the truck right there, but I couldn't give up a ride it had taken us so long to get.

Zogang is even wilder than Markam. Here the Khampas wear elaborate earrings, rings, necklaces, and huge metal lockets filled with magic potions. They sit around open fires along the street, surrounded by furs and hanging animal carcasses. They stare at us constantly but are open and friendly to foreigners and share our distrust of the Chinese.

The Khampas remind me of the Rastafarians from Jamaica. Dark and often wild-haired, they exude confidence and show little desire to be part of the rigid society set up by the Chinese. Fifty years ago, the Khampas were thieves and stole from nomads, travelers, and pilgrims. Now they make their living trading with the same people.

Khampa traders on Zogang's main and only street

They are savvy traders and hang out on the main street, selling jewelry and various natural medicines. Some of them become, by Chinese standards, quite rich.

Above the town of Zogang there are also some wonderful mountains, and I wanted to go hiking today. Unfortunately, it's pouring rain again, and quite cold, so here I sit on the bed in my hotel while rain drips on me through the leaky roof. It would have been a painful walk anyway, since the blisters on my heels are infected again. *Dukkha*! I spent two hours soaking my feet in hot salt water last night while I ate some canned fruit with Debbie and Monika.

The transportation situation is getting increasingly complicated. There are suddenly eight more foreigners in town, each with his or her own plans and needs. There are many confusing and conflicting rumors going around about which routes are open and which are blocked by landslides, where to get any kind of transportation at all, how long it will take, and how much money it will cost. We tried to rent a truck yesterday and went through innumerable changes in plans. It finally fell through when we found out the driver had been pulling our leg the entire time and never intended to rent us his truck at all.

Debbie's and Monika's visas will soon run out. They might be able to get them extended along the route if they go to the authorities. They might also be ignored, fined, arrested, or deported from China. In practice, Chinese bureaucracy has no rules. Everything depends on which officials you encounter and what mood they're in. As it is, Debbie and Monika are now waiting to get a truck ride on their own, and I may never see them again.

A few days later—I've lost track of the date

I've been singing Bob Dylan's "A Hard Rain's Gonna Fall," but I never thought it would fall this hard. I wanted badly to hike into the mountains, but the rain never stopped. It never stops—cold, wet, gray, continuous rain, day and night. Yesterday, I finally got fed up with being stuck in Zogang. Hitchhiking certainly wasn't getting me anywhere, and Debbie and Monika hadn't gotten anywhere either. So when I began to walk down the road, Debbie decided to join me. Monika stayed to wait for a ride—in either direction. She didn't care anymore.

It felt good to be back on the road. The rain slowed and then stopped, which was fortunate since my umbrella had been stolen in Zogang. We even got a ride in a truck for a few miles. By evening there was some blue sky and a few moments of sunshine, and when the clouds finally lifted, they revealed snow-capped mountains all around us. At last I felt charged with the energy and enthusiasm for adventure that had brought me here in the first place. We stopped in a small village and were invited to spend the night with a family right away. We couldn't refuse this offer for practical and diplomatic reasons, but it was a beautiful star-filled, crisp, moonlit evening, and it seemed a shame to spend it indoors. I consoled myself by planning an early morning hike.

The couple we stayed with had two small children and curious neighbors who came over to examine us. They had fun looking at my photos, inspecting our Western gadgets, and giving us language lessons. They laughed as Debbie and I practiced making *tsampa*. The Tibetans make it look like an art form, but I'm happy if I can just keep from spilling it all over the floor.

By morning the same drizzling, ugly, freezing rain
we thought we'd left behind had caught up to us again.
I love almost every form of weather—calm or stormy,
hot or cold—but I can't take this never-ending rain.
Because of this rain we are constantly wet and cold.
Because of this rain the road has washed out, so there's no
possibility of getting a truck ride. Worst of all, because of
this rain I'm not able to do the thing I want to do most—to
go trekking. I am in the most beautiful mountains I've ever
seen, but the magnificent peaks are all obscured by clouds.
I may as well be in some dismal, urban warehouse district
for all the nature I'm encountering. To be this close to what
I love—to have it right in front me and all around me—and
still be denied, this is truly *dukkha*! This is the heart of the
problem in my life. The normal patterns of living, of
deciding what I want and pursuing it, always seem to end
just short of the goal. There is always something lacking,
something hollow.

I'm beginning to feel this entire journey has been
cursed, that it is karmic retribution for some awful deed I
committed in the past. I've had bad luck every step of the
way. Road conditions, health, police, and weather have all
been against me. Someone even stole my toilet paper—I
had diarrhea at the time, of course. You can't buy toilet
paper around here, and I had to resort to my notebook
paper.

Finally, my patience and hope are fading, and I'm
filled with despair. I'm ready to give up all my plans, and
now I just want to get out of here. And how do I do that? I
will have to leave the one semi-dry spot I found by the side
of the road and go trudging on, blisters stinging, through
this freezing rain.

Next day   Semi-dry but still cold

I don't know why I keep allowing myself to become so frustrated, angry and depressed. I should know better. I should calmly watch my suffering and let it go. I need to have enough mindfulness, enough awareness to recognize *dukkha* when it arises and quickly let it go. How exasperating it must be for meditation masters to teach us when we refuse to take their simple advice to let go of the pain.

Next day

Yesterday and today have been better. It has hardly rained in two days! It's still overcast and chilly most of the time, but it seems like paradise.

Yesterday morning I took a walk up in the green hills near the road maintenance building where we'd slept. Even though I had an adrenalin-inducing standoff (or should I say "run off," which is what I did, quickly) with a couple of yak bulls, it was the most relaxing time I've had in quite a while. I only walked a short way from the road, but I could feel weeks of accumulated tension slipping away.

Shortly afterwards, Debbie and I got a ride on a tractor, and what a spectacular ride it was. The clouds had lifted, and we finally saw some awesome scenery—huge, snow-covered jagged peaks stretching far into the distance. Unfortunately, the tractor broke down after ten miles. A pin came loose and the entire back section fell off. We had to wait six hours for it to be repaired.

We walked to a nearby village to wait, but it was a real drag. Everyone tried to sell us things we didn't want. One shifty-looking fellow hovered around us like a vulture and the kids were obnoxius. We chased them away when their wheedling grew unbearable, and we told some people, point blank, to "shove it" in English, Swiss-German, Chinese, and Tibetan. I finally left and hiked up to the ruins of an old monastery.

We were back on the road as the sun set and passed more and more spectacular scenery. When the truck dropped us off before turning into a valley, Debbie and I had to wade through a flooded section of the road to get to a building that housed road maintenance workers. We convinced a family there to let us sleep on their floor. At first they hesitated, but after I showed them my phony document, they were quite impressed and became very friendly.

This area is much poorer than Yunnan Province. For the first time people are accepting the money I offer them in exchange for food and a place to sleep. The food, though, is of poor quality. We haven't seen any cheese or vegetable dishes for a long time. I keep thinking about the health food restaurant where I worked in New York City.

Tibetan girls

There, we threw away enough leftover food in a day to feed this family for a month. Here, everyone survives on rice, *tsampa*, and butter tea. Tibetans seem to live on this brew, sometimes drinking dozens of cups a day. I've drunk so much of this stuff it's made my sweat oily and greased up my insides.

The next morning we gave the family four *yuan* (80 cents) and a picture of the Dalai Lama; then Debbie and I set off down the road toward the town of Bamda. We are now at a pleasant spot by the river, and the sun has come out! At this moment everything seems beautiful and we are happy. We ate a jar of mandarin oranges we had been saving and relaxed by the side of the road.

It's good traveling with a companion. We joke a lot and support each other psychologically. It's also practical. One of us can explore while the other one watches the luggage. Of course, we tell everyone that we're married (they all ask), and the people are completely perplexed when we tell them we have no children. They also want to know who's taking care of our sheep, chickens, and yaks while we're away.

Evening   Bamda

From our sunny spot by the river we got a ride to Bamda, which consists of a parking lot, an army hotel, and two restaurants built around a fork in the road. Here, despite all the good reasons I just outlined for traveling together, Debbie and I decided to split company. The truck that brought us to Bamda was continuing north to Chamdo. Going this way Debbie might make it to Lhasa (620 miles away) before her visa expires. I still want to take the more scenic southern route, even though the road is washed out and blocked by landslides. It was a sad parting, but I think we both made the right decision.

My route from Bamda went directly over a high pass. It wasn't raining, so I just started walking. Since the road was blocked and there was no possibility of getting a ride on a truck, I left the long switchbacks of the road and took the steeper, more direct, foot-paths used by yak herders. It was great to be on a mountain trail instead of that stinking road.

I was surrounded by steep, green hills dotted with yaks and herds of sheep, and I even came across some wildlife—marmots, jack rabbits, and flocks of birds—that had escaped the machine guns of Chinese soldiers. Wildlife has been nearly exterminated as a result of the Chinese incursion.

It felt great to reach the top of the pass by footpower, and I was rewarded by the sight of a whole string of saw-toothed, snow-covered peaks. Prayer flags marking the pass waved in the breeze, and a herd of yaks stared at me in surprise. I worked my way down the other side and set up my tent next to a rushing stream. The sky looks like it might bring some rain tonight, but for now, it's beautiful.

Next day

It did rain last night. My Hong Kong bivy sack kept me semi-dry. Today it only rained half the time, and I consider myself lucky.

I walked down the valley all day and stopped to have *tsampa* and butter tea with a friendly, intelligent, good-looking Khampa. I gave him a picture of the Dalai Lama, and when he saw who it was, he undid his long hair and reverently touched the top of his head with the photo.

Khampa horseman

Further down the valley I came upon an entire village harvesting barley. The men sang while the women worked. Khampa men have it pretty good. They are in charge of drinking tea, talking politics, looking handsome,

Khampa woman at barley harvest

and acting macho. All this keeps them quite busy, so the women take care of the heavy labor and hard work.

I sat for a while with some kids at a big *chorten*, which is a religious monument built out of stone with a square base and a round spire. These monuments house holy relics or scriptures. A very old couple walked around and around the *chorten*, chanting and praying with their strings of prayer beads.

I continued on down the mountain foot-paths marked by stones engraved with Tibetan script. These markers are called mani-stones, because the inscription is often the *om mani padme hum* mantra. Sometimes the letters are a foot high on the faces of huge boulders, and sometimes a rock is covered by one-inch-high lettering so perfect, it looks as if it had been printed with a press. I've read that there used to be ancient markers of this type on the main roads as well, but the Chinese smashed them up to use as gravel.

Tonight I'm staying under a bridge and am happy that I'll be dry if it rains. I feel relaxed and am singing a song of John Lennon, "I'm just sittin' here watching the wheels go round and round. I love to watch them roll. No longer riding on that merry-go-round, I just had to let it go."

August 16 Bashu

Yesterday I walked down to what I think was the Salween River valley. The hot, dry road along the river was unpleasant, and it was frequently broken by landslides.

It was the longest day of walking I've had so far, and I was exhausted by the end of it. Luckily I happened upon a group of road workers with two trucks who were willing to take me the last 20 miles to Bashu. I was happy with the prospect of a good meal and a bed to recuperate in.

Once I got to town I was surprised to find five Westerners and stayed up late talking and drinking with them. I got on well with three of them, but they left this morning, on foot, to Bamda. The other two were lazy and complained incessantly. Even so, I found myself clinging to their company.

Today I'm feeling weak and sickly. It's like my body is collapsing. I ate several big meals at the restaurants in town to try to gain back some weight. I'm so thin that my pants keep slipping down over my hips.

This town isn't as primitive as Markam or Zogang. The food is better, and the people are more sedate. The area is dry and beautiful and looks like the American Southwest with white peaks in the background. The colors of the hills are startling—gold, pink, and purple. Tomorrow I want to hike up to the forest, but I don't know whether I'll have the energy. "You know you're over the hill when your mind makes promises your body can't fill." (Lowell George of Little Feat)

August 18 Rawu

Yesterday I wasn't feeling well enough for hiking, so I decided to see if I could get onward transportation. Without much waiting I got a ride on an old tractor for 30 miles. The trip, however, took over ten hours. Loaded with passengers and baggage, we crawled uphill at little more than a walking pace and stopped half a dozen times at practically every village along the way so the driver and other passengers could visit with friends.

It was a great way to see the countryside. Unfortunately I was feeling very nauseous. I began to feel like a bottle of beer that had been shaken vigorously. At every bump (and there were a lot of them), I thought I was going to explode. To make matters worse, one man who took a liking to me was a heavy drinker. He kept pushing his bottle of *jiu* on me and telling me what a good friend I was. I felt obligated to drink a little with him, and this made me feel even worse. By the time the ride ended it was dark, a cold wind was blowing, and I felt horrible. I managed to set up my tent, moaning and groaning with an aching, gas-filled belly, and lay down for a night disturbed by rain, cold, and toilet runs every half hour.

I haven't pinned down what causes these bouts of sickness, and I keep hoping I'm building up some kind of immunity. Yesterday was the worst so far, and I was worried that something was seriously wrong with me. But this morning I woke up feeling okay, and after plugging up my tubes with *tsampa, mountons* (heavy bread), noodles and rice, I soon got a ride for the last 25 miles to Rawu.

This area is everything I had hoped it would be and more. The little town of Rawu is dwarfed by a huge lake which is surrounded by green meadows filled with horses, cows, yaks, and sheep. And all around, the mountains are incredible. Today I walked through pine forests and flowering meadows, and found a lake hidden in the hills. I'm reminded of the Sierras in California, where I spent a summer as a forest ranger. But the pointed peaks rising everywhere leave no doubt I'm in the Himalayas.

After my walk I saw three monks doing prostrations along the road. From a standing position they fell forward with outstretched arms, then lowered themselves until their foreheads touched the ground. They stood up and repeated the process from the point where their hands last touched the ground. One of them looked to be about ten years old. This young boy was a novice, sort of a monk-in-training. When he's about twenty, he will ordain as a full monk.

The monks told me they are on a pilgrimage to Lhasa, and each day they do full prostrations equal to the number of kilometers they are from their goal. Prostrations are an expression of their faith and a way to gain merit. At Rawu these monks are still 750 kilometers (465 miles) away from Lhasa and so had to do 750 prostrations today. And they had already come 800 kilometers! For obvious reasons, they were very interested in the distances listed in my guidebook.

Monk and novice on pilgrimage to Lhasa

Today I'm feeling like my old self for the first time in a long time and am glad circumstances conspired to keep me going instead of turning me back when I was feeling so pessimistic last week. I'm looking forward to getting in shape through hiking and to getting to know the people in this area. I'll just keep my fingers crossed that this cool, comfortable, dry weather lasts.

August 19 (or thereabouts)

This morning I felt rather ill again, but I think I've pinned down one of the culprits of my gastric pain and diarrhea. It's the powdered milk I've been drinking. I've heard that Asian milk powder is made from ingredients that were contaminated by the Chernobyl nuclear reactor accident and rejected in Europe.

Even though I felt weak, I hiked up to an impressive waterfall on the road to Zayu and found a generous patch of sunny blue sky. I stretched out in a grassy spot and soaked up the warm sunshine for about thirty minutes. At this altitude, that's all the naked exposure to the sun I could take before getting burned. So now I'm sitting in the chilly shade of a rock outcropping trying to hang on to the last ghost of warmth. I'm feeling energetic once again.

August 20

As I walked back to Rawu last night I happily debated with myself about which mountain peak I would climb today. But when today arrived, I was content to spend nearly all day reading in bed, napping, and EATING. I have finally found a shop that sells something besides Chinese sugar biscuits and puffed rice bars and bought myself canned mandarin oranges, peanuts, and nougat bars so sweet I could feel my teeth start to rot. I had frightful visions of ending up in the chair of a road-side dentist in Lhasa who uses a fifty-year-old drill powered by a foot pedal, but that didn't stop me. It was a real pigout, and it was great.

It has been a difficult trip up to now and has taken a lot of physical and mental strength. I knew this route would be tough, possibly dangerous, and that it was definitely illegal, but I wouldn't have been satisfied riding on a bus, zipping blindly through the spectacular scenery, bypassing all the interesting little towns, and missing the opportunity to get to know these people and their culture.

Rawu has helped recharge my batteries some, but I would really like to get to Lhasa for a more thorough recuperation. And so, I will probably leave here tomorrow. Maybe Debbie will be there, and Doug should be arriving around the first of September from Japan. It will be good to see a familiar face.

August 21

This morning I got a ride on a tractor that took me about ten miles before the front tire blew. We skidded perilously close to the edge of the cliff before stopping. The driver simply abandoned the vehicle and walked back to town. It's a good thing I felt stronger today, because I ended up hiking the next 12 miles. The road followed a white water river (not a muddy red one, like most of the ones I've seen) through a gorgeous valley where incredible waterfalls plummeted down steep canyon walls. Deep green pine forests covered the slopes, and snowy peaks rose all around me. Things here are so much bigger than in the mountains back home.

I finally got another tractor ride from some friendly road workers, and we picked up logs, equipment, and people all along the way. By the time we got to the road maintenance station, the tractor looked like a clown wagon.

I was invited to spend the night at the station, and after dinner, I sang for the children and had them all clap to the beat of various songs. "Puff the Magic Dragon" was a favorite, but they were just as enthusiastic about "Psycho Killer." Now everyone's sitting around the main room, and it's time for some *chang*, the Tibetan beer made from barley. Tomorrow the tractor will continue to Bomi, which is also known as Zhamo. This is a stroke of luck; Bomi is nearly 60 miles away. Naturally, the tractor has no shock absorbers, so I expect to be thoroughly shaken up by the end of the day.

August 22 Bomi

We got an early start this morning and rolled through some of the most magnificent scenery I've ever seen. Pine trees clung precariously from huge rock walls that towered over the road, and peaks reached into the sky at unbelievable angles. Hiking through these ranges would be a monumental accomplishment. Scaling these walls would be a climber's dream. I could hardly contain myself. I felt overwhelmed by the beauty and was actually relieved when we moved on to scenery that was only spectacular instead of awe-inspiring.

We were driving alongside a cascading stream when we came upon a group of trucks, tractors, and jeeps parked in the middle of the road. Everyone was standing and looking into a huge hole, fifteen feet deep and twenty feet wide, where the road used to cross the river. It was impassable even on foot. I was ready to give up, but some of the other drivers calmly began to make a new road crossing further up stream. Once it was ready, our driver went for this new route without hesitation. The passengers had to push, pull, and carry the tractor over boulders, up the steep embankment, and through the stream, all the way to the other side of the washout. All the tractors like ours made it across, and the passengers from the trucks and jeeps that didn't climbed aboard the vehicles that did. We ended up with fourteen people and all their luggage on our tiny tractor. With the other tractors similarly loaded, we lumbered off down the road like a parade, and there was a feeling of celebration in the air.

The driver dropped me off on the outskirts of Bomi because he was worried about the authorities seeing a foreigner on his tractor. I walked the last mile into town and was amazed at how big it was. I had gotten used to one-street towns with just a few shops. But Bomi is a metropolis. It has a barber, a dentist, and restaurants with more than two tables. The shops sell all sorts of items that I haven't seen since Lijiang, like toothpaste and film. I walked up and down the street merrily gorging myself on sweets. Bomi's elevation is around 9000 feet, and there are beautiful mountains surrounding the town. I think I'll spend tomorrow immersed in their shadows.

August 23

So much for my plans for a walk. It is pouring rain outside, a cold, ugly, continuous rain from thick, low, gray clouds that hide any hint of the nearby mountains. So I'm stuck here in my hotel room, for which I was charged the foreign rate, five *yuan* ($1.00)—twice what the Chinese pay.

I now have time to describe some of the local habits I've picked up in my travels. Although I'm not as proficient as the Chinese in spitting or blowing my nose without benefit of a handkerchief, I have learned how to eat Chinese/Tibetan style. Talking with one's mouth full of food is a legitimate way to conduct dinner conversation. And one should also grunt and snort while stuffing in the food as fast as possible. When the locals come across a bone or something distasteful, they simply spit it on the floor for the chickens and pigs who will wander in later to clean it up. A few loud belches are the polite way to punctuate a meal.

Tibetan toilet habits have taken longer to get used to. The locals are only slightly more discriminating in this than they are in where they choose to spit. The public toilets consist mainly of a hole in a concrete floor. But it seems at least half the people miss the hole, sometimes by as much as two feet. Of course, that may be so they can steer clear of the little white worms that live in the frothing, putrid stew below and that crawl upward at the sight of human flesh. The toilets are rarely, if ever, cleaned. Needless to say, I never walk to the toilet barefoot. Toilet paper, as we know it, is nonexistent. Almost any paper product will do—newspaper, magazine pages, notebook paper, old letters, receipts, and, especially, used cigarette packs. I've also seen pages from school books.

The public toilets are only used half the time, how-ever. There are no private toilets, but for Tibetans any ditch, bush, rock, or alley will do. Under the cover of night they are even less bashful. I woke up this morning and found a fresh pile of human excrement in the parking lot outside my hotel room. Eventually it will solidify and the rain will mix it with the surrounding mud and refuse. I have to admit that I have, on occasion, been equally indiscreet, especially during my bouts of diarrhea. In Bashu, one time, I just crossed the street to a blank wall and squatted like a chicken while people walked by. I'll definitely have to amend some of these new habits before I get home.

August 25 Tangmai

Yesterday morning I set off walking. I had no choice—the truck drivers were afraid to give a ride to a foreigner and wouldn't touch me with a ten-foot pole. I even held a wad of bills in my hand and approached a driver fixing a flat tire, but he just waved me off. He wouldn't look me in the eye, much less read my document. Fortunately, I had the energy to walk and set a goal for myself of 15 miles.

Just as I reached my goal, a big, Western-style tractor with a wagon trailer came along. I hopped in the back and was off for a great ride through the forest. Many of the trees were changing color, and the crisp, energizing feel of autumn was in the air. Then, as we continued to descend in altitude, everything turned tropical. We stopped at a road house for the night, and I slept in the woodshed Woody Guthrie style—with my "bed on the floor."

Today I reached Tangmai after a brief tractor ride and a ten-mile walk. Tangmai has one big hotel, two restaurants and some huts and houses scattered through the hills. Besides a few hotel workers, there seem to be no permanent residents. With the road blocked and no vehicles coming through, it feels like a ghost town.

I was able to get some hot water for a sponge bath and to soak my feet. The low altitude, about 5500 feet, means hot weather and my hefty, steel-toed army boots are more uncomfortable than ever. I've been trying to buy a pair of Chinese sneakers, which all the Tibetans wear, but I can't find a pair big enough.

After my bath I walked down the road to a large bridge where a very old man with a rifle was standing guard. There was a sandy beach under the bridge, so I took off my shirts and shoes to lie in the sand and rejuvenate my body and mind with some sunshine. Immediately, the guard began to yell and some young Chinese soldiers from a nearby barracks came running down to the beach.

They told me I couldn't stay there because the bridge might be bombed! Bombed? By whom? I wondered. I knew that China and India were fighting along their border, but I had not heard of any bombings this far inland. However, in Rawu I had seen truckloads of young Chinese soldiers heading down the road toward Zayu. What this earth needs, I decided, is a "Buddhist jihad": a holy peace.

I was willing to take my chances of being bombed for the opportunity to bask in the sun, but the Chinese are the most persistent people in the world, and eventually I had to relent. The soldiers invited me into their barracks for candy, tea, and apples, a conciliatory gesture I would have appreciated more if I hadn't regretted wasting a sunny afternoon.

I felt like eating constantly today. Unfortunately, there's not much to buy in this town except noodles and peanuts. Thoughts of Lhasa, rumored to be a veritable smorgasbord of a town, make my mouth water. But Lhasa is still nearly 350 miles away. Once I leave Tangmai, I will hit an infamous section of road that is washed out nearly all summer and fall. I have plenty more walking to look forward to.

August 26   Somewhere between Tangmai and Linzhi

I don't know how many miles I walked today. There were no road markers and often no road.

When I set out this morning, the sky was clear and I was feeling strong, even though the air was hot and steamy. The vegetation along the road was wild and thick with ferns, bamboo, and vines twisted around trees of infinite variety. I followed a wide, swollen, and riotous river with roaring rapids swirling, churning, and slamming recklessly into huge rocks.

After walking a few miles I reached the section where the road was blocked. First there were numerous small landslides where fallen trees and boulders littered the road. Then I came to a huge rock, as big as my parents' two-story home in California, that had fallen from the side of the mountain above into the middle of the road. Past that was a section where the entire mountainside had collapsed and created huge mudslides 150 to 200 feet across and so steep that I could look straight down 300 feet to the rushing river below. Between the mudslides there were big cracks in the road where it looked as though it might give way at any moment. I followed some footsteps in the mud and kept looking up for falling rocks. And if I slipped off the trail, I would never be able to climb back up. About then it began to rain.

The "road" worked its way down toward a tributary stream, where it simply disappeared. The only way to cross the water was on a contraption Westerners call the "flying fox." A metal cable stretched from one side of the stream to the other and had a narrow bar to sit on. The caretaker came out of his little shack to collect his fee and helped me climb aboard. He gave a shove and I whizzed over the river far below. Once I was safely on the other side, he sent my pack flying after me.

Now it's pouring rain again. I'm sitting under my tarp tied between two trees on the beach by the river. There may be road houses further on, but I'm too exhausted to continue. If I can manage to stay dry, this will be a good place to spend the night.

August 27

Today has generally been horrible. The rain continued non-stop last night and left me soaked and covered with fine, wet sand from the beach. I hardly slept. Weak and exhausted, I continued walking today. There were no trucks or tractors, and I made little progress.

By nightfall I found a hotel for food and a dry bed, but I'm the only one staying here since there are no vehicles on the road. Some friendly Tibetans live in the adjacent houses. They tried to marry me off to a short, fat girl.

I've been trying to learn Tibetan, but it's nearly useless since every area has a radically different dialect. Many times I've memorized words only to find them received with puzzled looks 50 miles down the road.

I need a decent night's sleep. Last night there was the rain; the night before that there was lots of noise and commotion in the hotel; before that I was on a woodshed floor; before that I had Sichuan roommates who stayed up late—yelling and howling with laughter—and on and on. I can't remember the last time I slept well.

August 28

I knew it was going to be a good day when I woke up this morning and saw it wasn't raining. A few miles down the road, I met two Tibetans with big loads on their backs. The younger one told me that he and his uncle were traveling to Bayi past Linzhi and I could join them if I wished. They already had a ride lined up going to a logging town 25 miles away. From there I might be able to get a ride all the way to Lhasa! While we waited for the truck we drank hot butter tea, ate snacks, and listened to Tibetan music on a Chinese boombox.

The truck turned out to be another old relic. The radiator leaked constantly and we had to stop at every stream to refill it. At one point, the driver asked whether anyone had any soap. I thought he just wanted to wash the grease off his hands, so I gave him mine. When I looked again, I saw that he had torn up the bar and was using it to plug the radiator. Tibetan soap must be made from lard or something more water-resistant than my Western soap because it clearly didn't work very well and the radiator continued to leak.

We shared the truck with half a dozen playful local girls and women who gave me my first taste of the rock-hard Tibetan cheese. The Tibetans will gnaw on a chunk for hours, the way we chew gum.

By mid-day it began to rain again, and we soon came upon a bulldozer and road crew clearing the inevitable landslide. This one was still in progress and a continuous stream of mud with an occasional goopy mess of rocks slipped down the hillside and onto the road. Every ten or fifteen minutes a huge boulder would bounce by at an astonishing speed. This was serious business. The boulders were big enough and fast enough to smash a truck. The road crew had rock spotters perched along the hill.

When one of them yelled that a boulder was on its way, the bulldozer would rush backwards to safety. We were there for about two hours; then we took turns running across the danger zone. The driver followed us in the truck at full speed.

We arrived at the logging town just as the sun was setting. It is located at the top of a 16,000-foot pass, above a beautiful valley filled with streams and green meadows and surrounded by snowy peaks, all highlighted by a clear, blue sky. My new friends and I went for a walk through town, and what did we find but a full court basketball game in progress. The players invited me to fill in and I happily accepted. I must have been quite a sight running around in my heavy boots and my Khampa hat, breathless from the altitude. Lucky for me they didn't know much about driving the lane and certainly didn't know how to defend it.

Every truck driver we met tonight said he'll be leaving tomorrow. I'll soon be in Lhasa and right on schedule to meet Doug. I believe—knock on wood—that my poor old feet are done walking.

August 29 Bayi

I'm lovin' it baby, I'm lovin' it. After an early truck ride to Linzhi, I left my friends and took a bus to Bayi. There I was told that all bus tickets on to Lhasa, 250 miles away, were sold out. Then, once again, I ran into the ever-diligent *Gong An*. It's their duty to make sure that foreigners leave closed areas within twenty-four hours, and they normally send them back to the town they came from. All I had to do was tell them that I had come from Lhasa to be assured a seat on the next bus to Lhasa.

The chief of police was very polite. He told me, in halting, phrasebook English, "Mr. Jim, I tell you, this is not an open area. You must go back to Lhasa as soon as possible."

The waiting, the hustling for truck rides, the frustration of broken promises and miscommunications—it's all over. The police found me a hotel room to wait in since they're not sure when the bus will get here. All I have to do now is relax and sit in the sunshine of the hotel courtyard. Someone will come to get me when the bus arrives.

3

LHASA

Don't waste your energy traveling in search
Of the eternal bliss you hope for in the world.
Looking for the turtle's beard, you'll die for nothing.
True happiness doesn't run after the world
And is above every stream of pain and sorrow.

Buddhadasa Bhikkhu

September 1 Lhasa

I made it! The sun was shining when the bus pulled
onto the paved road at the edge of Lhasa, and I could see
the massive Potala Palace, the ancient home of the Dalai
Lama, sitting on top of a hill overlooking the city.

The bus ride had been more than a little trying. The
driver charged me twice the local rate and then refused to
let me have a seat. So for two days, I had to ride on the
engine cover next to him. The bus was the most rickety,
rundown excuse for a vehicle I've ever seen. Everything
but everything was broken, patched, ripped, dented, and
held together with tape and wire. Every time the bus
stopped, the engine stalled. The driver, muttering Tibetan
curses, would get out and crank start it with a long rod,
and every few hours he had to go under the hood or
beneath the bus to get it running again. Once, when it was
raining, the driver suddenly pulled to a stop and, sputter-
ing gibberish, ran back down the road to get his wind-
shield wiper which had fallen off.

The first thing I did in Lhasa was to go to the post
office. News from my family was sweet to read. I crave

the little pieces of home my mother and grandparents send me in their letters. The news from Doug was not so sweet; he won't be coming to Lhasa after all. He said he didn't think the Chinese would let him bring his mountain bike into Tibet. So he's going to meet me in Kathmandu in a month instead. Now I have no plans.

I wanted to find Debbie and Monika as soon as possible. They were the only people who could understand what I'd just been through. I checked all the hotels for notes on the message boards, and looked in *post restante* (general delivery) for messages, but found nothing. I was on my way back to my hotel, a little worried for them, when I took a quick look in the Yak Hotel. There on the wall was an envelope with the message, "Jim, we're at the Banak Shol, Deb & Mon."

I found Debbie right away, and Monika soon joined us. We exchanged stories in a rush of excited happiness. They had been reunited along the northern route, which had taken them only three days less than my long and slow southern route. We were very glad to be in Lhasa.

September 2

I've discovered that Lhasa has the all the usual disadvantages of a big city. Everyone tries to rip us off in the marketplace, and the hotel prices are much higher than they were in the country, almost $3.00 a night. People here are also much more reserved, more closed and suspicious. Seedy characters abound, as do litter, noise, and foul smells. Huge numbers of Chinese civilians have been moved into Tibet, and they now outnumber Tibetans, so most of the city is Chinese. They have built block after block of ugly, low-budget, modern concrete eyesores.

At first Lhasa looked as bad as it did good. However, now that my clothes and my body are clean at last and I'm eating fresh fruits, vegetables, yogurt, and lots of yak burgers, it's beginning to look much better.

Our hotel, the Banak Shol, is in the Tibetan part of the city, near the Jokhang, the oldest monastery in Lhasa and Tibet's most sacred temple. Here the buildings have colorfully painted and carved windows, lintels, and eaves. The narrow, winding streets are bounded by the high white walls of the irregularly shaped houses. White banners with appliquéd blue designs hang in all the doorways.

September 3

It was sunny today, so everyone was out and in a good mood, including Debbie, Monika and me. We saw pilgrims chanting and performing prostrations in front of the Jokhang, while ten-foot tall, oven-like incense burners billowed clouds of gray smoke. A huge crowd of people gathered around a filthy little man with matted hair, who was dressed in untanned leather. He was a cross between a street performer and a crazy saint and was throwing hot water, yogurt, and what I suppose were yak intestines at anyone who ventured too close. He dashed toward the crowd with a yak's head in his hand and muttered insanely, as the Tibetans ran away howling with laughter.

The oldest part of the Jokang was built in the seventh century. Just outside the temple sit two huge prayer wheels, which are wooden drums containing scrolls inscribed with prayers. The faithful spin the cylinders to release the prayers and earn merit toward a higher rebirth in the next life. Inside, the temple is filled with statues and chapels dedicated to various Buddhist deities. Hundreds of lamps fueled with yak butter constantly burn. From the roof, we had a good view of the Barkhor, the circular road that surrounds the Jokhang.

The Barkhor is both a pilgrimage circuit and a bazaar. It is the heart of Tibetan life in Lhasa, and we spent the afternoon exploring it. We wandered past monks sitting in the street chanting for donations. We were pestered by women loaded down with turquoise, coral, and silver jewelry, real and fake, who kept asking us "how mucha" we wanted to pay for their wares. We saw a dirty, tattered man dragging himself along on crutches doing prostrations in the middle of the roving crowd. Above him, kids were flying kites. I was approached by a group of *"kuchee, kuchee"* ("please, please") girls who begged me for money, then food, then Dalai Lama pictures which they probably planned to

Jewelry sales in the Barkhor bazaar

resell at exorbitant prices. We walked past stalls lining the street that offered everything a Tibetan (or tourist) could ever need. In the food market, we saw fifty-pound wheels of butter, gunny sacks full of barley flour, and chunks of yak meat, limbs, fur, and guts. The sight of bloody yak heads discarded in the street nearly made me sick.

The air was filled with the yells of hawkers, Tibetan music, Western music, chanting, the beat of drums, dozens of languages and local dialects, and the ringing of bells on bicycles trying to squeeze through the crowd.

Overcome by all this activity, we escaped to a small *chang* tent with a single table and a few benches. The beer was served from a teapot by the *chang* woman, who refilled our teacups as many times as we wanted for only a few cents. I really enjoy the tangy, slightly bitter taste of Tibetan beer.

On a clear day the mountains surrounding Lhasa look close enough to touch. Other times they seem unreal, like a backdrop for a stage. Today we were treated to a brilliant double rainbow arching over the city with every color clearly defined.

But the Potala Palace dominates the landscape. Its red-brown and white buildings soar thirteen stories high. Before the Chinese takeover, the Potala had been the main residence of the Dalai Lama and the bureaucratic center of Tibetan religion and politics since the seventeenth century. Now it's a tourist site. It stirs up a strange mix of feelings in me. It has the ancient and forbidding power of a medieval castle but it also represents the mystery and magic of Tibetan religion. I can hardly take my eyes off it.

Potala Palace, ancient home of the Dalai Lama

September 4

Last night Debbie asked me to tell her why I wanted to become a monk, something I had only casually mentioned to her before. I told her how I was introduced to Buddhism in college and immediately felt that it was a way of life that made sense to me. Many people become interested in Buddhism and meditation after a personal tragedy or during a painful period in their lives. But I was generally quite happy. I loved life and I felt loved. Yet I sensed that life had something better to offer, that it was somehow not what it pretended to be.

I began to practice Zen Buddhist meditation, I told her, but I was still searching for answers.

I asked my Zen teacher, Katagiri Roshi, "If I <u>think</u> I'm happy, what's the problem? Why do I need to practice meditation? Even if my happiness is a delusion, why not be content to live it? Maybe ignorance really <u>is</u> bliss."

"You're suffering," he would answer.

I can see now that I was suffering, but at the time my mindfulness was not keen enough to understand. I was unknowingly perpetuating cycles of stress and conflict in my life. It was only later, after I'd deepened my practice of meditation, that I began to recognize these cycles as *dukkha*, and to see that letting go of *dukkha* would bring true happiness.

The Buddha's teachings offer a way, the Noble Eight-Fold Path, to completely eliminate this suffering. It culminates in *Nibbana [Nirvana]*— enlightenment, the perfect peace. *Nibbana* actually means "cool," the ultimate cool. And until I reach *Nibbana*, I will always be subject to *dukkha*.

As a monk, I explained, I can totally devote myself to following the Path. This way I hope to eliminate my feelings of discontent, live in harmony with my surroundings, and find inner peace through wisdom and understanding.

Debbie listened carefully, but I could see she was trying to reconcile the wild traveler sitting in front of her with the image of me as a bald-headed, brown-robed, barefoot monk.

This trip has become more than just another adventure for me. I set out to experience "*dukkha* travel," travel too full of discomfort to be ignored. I wanted to push myself to the limits and confront my own demons, and I have not been disappointed. This trip has been full of sickness, pain, and dissatisfaction. What I've discovered is that when I don't fight the discomfort, when I let it go, my suffering is less. When I accept the problems that arise, they lose their power over me. I'm gaining confidence that I'll be able to handle just about anything life sends my way.

But it's still hard to believe how close I am to giving up travel, women, and *chang*.

Lhasa monk

September 5

My plans are changing rapidly. Eating, drinking, and talking all day is starting to get to me. I've found some companions who want to go to Mt. Kailas, about 1300 miles away in western Tibet. It, along with Lake Manasarovar, is the most sacred place of pilgrimage for Hindus and Tibetan Buddhists.

If I go to Kailas, it will take me a lot longer to get to Kathmandu to meet Doug, but I could still make it by mid-October. One thing I've learned here is that it's impossible to plan more than a few days ahead. I keep telling myself, just go with the flow with an open mind. No expectations, no problems.

September 6

I spent the last few days running errands with my new Swedish traveling partner, Per. Debbie and Monika also plan to join us. We've been gathering the necessary information, food, supplies, and travel permits (authentic ones, this time, from the Public Security Bureau) for our trip. The area we're going to is sparsely populated, so we need to stock up.

Many of the hotels and restaurants in Lhasa that cater to Western travelers are virtual trading posts. The travelers' co-op in our hotel keeps a large book where people can write down advice and tips about places they've been. A big bulletin board in the lobby is crammed with cards proclaiming who has what to buy or sell and where they can be found. I bought another sleeping bag from a Polish guy who was about to ship out. It's a massive thing that, together with the light bag I already have, will surely keep me warm. Per bought a tent from a Danish traveler. I considered trading my bivy sack for a larger, sturdier tent, but decided against the extra weight and cost. With nothing more than my little tent, I'm more apt to approach the locals for an invitation to spend the night, especially when it rains. We are all stocking up on parkas, gloves, and boots. I am having a pair of Tibetan boots made because even in Lhasa they don't have any shoes my size.

I hate to leave Lhasa, but I can feel Kailas drawing me toward it.

September 8

Yesterday at lunch I heard about an American woman, Valerie, who is staying at the Lhasa Hotel, the most expensive place in town. She is planning to rent a

couple of trucks to drive to Mount Kailas. I immediately
went to find a Colombian I met a few days ago, who wants
to film a short documentary on Kailas and was also
looking for a ride.

We went to Valerie's hotel, hoping to convince her to
take us with her.

Valerie turned out to be very "spiritual." She invited
us for tea and told us that she decided to go to Kailas after
a number of "signs" indicated that it was her destiny to be
there. One of these signs was a book that fell off a shelf
and opened at a chapter on Kailas. She also told us that the
astrological charts indicated this was a prodigious time to
be in Tibet. Powerful male forces are apparently intersect-
ing with female forces in the Himalayas in a way that they
haven't in thousands of years. All of us, she said, have
been subconsciously drawn to this area to balance out
these conflicting forces. She also told us there's going to be
an eclipse that will be visible from Kailas on September 19.
This is all connected with the positive spiritual power of
the Dalai Lama and his return to Tibet, her past life as a
monk, the double rainbow, etc., etc.

We asked when she was leaving. She said she had
"meditated" and was told to leave September 11. She was
enthusiastic about giving us a ride and consulted her
Tibetan guide, who seemed to think it would not be a
problem. What unexpected luck: a truck, a guide, and an
eclipse! The positive forces were so strong, she said, that
all obstacles would be swept away.

We could hardly contain ourselves. We ran back to
the hotel to tell the others and a celebration immediately
ensued. Two Americans set up a big stereo on the top floor
of the Banak Shol and cranked out Talking Heads, the

Police, the Clash, and Bob Marley. A bunch of us danced, as wildly as we could at 12,000 feet, under a luminous full moon until five in the morning—all of us high on the prospect of traveling together to the holy mountain.

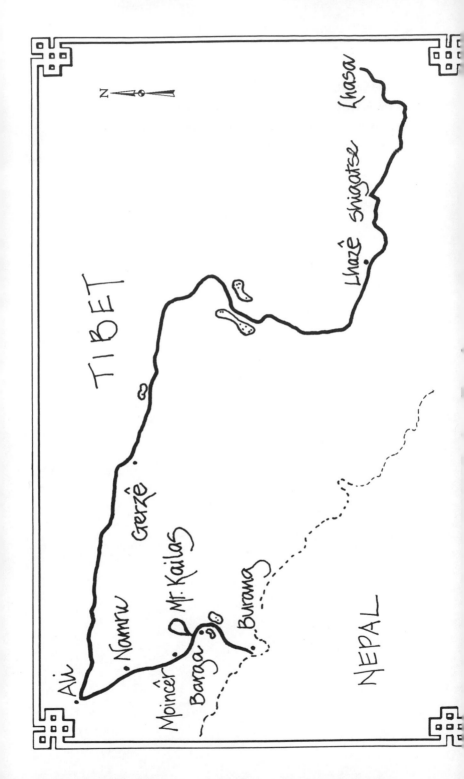

WESTERN TIBET

Sure it hurts. The trick is not minding that it hurts.
T. E. Lawrence

September 11

For three days everything revolved around organiz-
ing our ride with Valerie. Plans changed every day.
Change, change, change. What a burden! I kept thinking if
I was patient, everything would work out. Then yesterday
morning we ran up against the blank wall of the Chinese
Tourist Authority, who, at the last minute, denied us
permission to go with Valerie. They didn't even give us a
reason. So Valerie and her convoy went on its merry way
without us and we had to start all over again.

We found another truck at twice the price and
needed twice as many people to make it affordable. Per
and I realized that things were quickly getting out of hand.
The price of the truck was going up every hour, more and
more people were involved, and the arrangements were
growing impossibly complicated. The two of us decided to
return to our original plan and hitchhike. We'll see our
friends again at Kailas.

Over the past three days, I've been reminded repeatedly that everything is subject to change. *Anicca*, one of the
fundamental principles of Buddhism, says everything is
impermanent; all existence is transitory; nothing is stable or
permanently satisfying. *Anicca* is the underlying cause of
all *dukkha*, but it's also our only hope. "If it wasn't for

impermanence, we'd be stupid forever." (Ajahn Buddhadasa)

It was difficult to hitch a ride out of the city, so Per and I hopped on a bus for a 200-mile, twelve-hour, dust-filled, bucking bronco ride to Shigatse. At least I'm on the road again. Our pilgrimage to the holy mountain is underway, and it feels good.

September 12   Shigatse

We slept late this morning but found a truck that will leave tomorrow for Gerzê, about 550 miles away. From here on we'll have to rely totally on trucks; that's the only means of transportation available in western Tibet.

Shigatse is the second largest city in Tibet and the traditional home of the Panchen Lama, second in power only to the Dalai Lama. The present Panchen Lama was imprisoned by the Chinese for fourteen years and then required to live in Beijing, with only occasional visits permitted to his homeland.

Per in front of the Tashilhunpo Monastery in Shigatse

This afternoon we explored the Tashilhunpo Monastery, which is the Panchen Lama's official residence. I read that as many as 4000 monks once lived here, although only a few hundred remain. We wandered around the huge spread of buildings, then climbed to the top of the hill behind it where colorful prayer flags fluttered in the breeze. I tied my handkerchief among them.

September 14 On route

Yesterday morning we got up at 5:00 to meet our truck, which never came. We did, however, find another ride 90 miles to Lhazê where we took a small, flat-bottomed ferry across the Yarlung Tsang Po, known also by its Hindi name, the Brahmaputra River. Once on the other side, we found a truck willing to take us to Gerzê.

Last night we camped by the truck stop and cooked up a feast of a meal and shared it with some of the drivers. They supplied the *chang*. We were up again at 5:00 this morning in case our truck left early, but it's already 9:00, and the drivers and other passengers are still asleep.

We are now on the great Tibetan Plateau, the Chang Tang. The landscape here is completely different from that of eastern Tibet. The only sign of vegetation in these hills and valleys is a sparse covering of grass and thin crops of barley in rocky soil. Dust is a real problem. By the end of the day we are covered in it. I tied my bandana over my face like a bandit in order to breathe.

Same day around midnight

We began rolling about noon in a convoy of five big Isuzu trucks. All day long we rumbled through beautiful, green rolling hills and vast, grassy valleys. There were a few tiny settlements, but for the most part, all we saw in the way of people were nomad yak herders and hundreds of yaks.

I love this land. The hills roll on and on, and the sky is an endless deep blue. When the sun shines at this altitude, over 13,000 feet, everything glows and glistens.

The convoy stopped numerous times so the drivers and passengers could make tea. There was no wood to burn so they boiled water from the river by aiming a gasoline torch at the kettle. They sat on rugs and sheep skins and ate from half a carcass of dried sheep. The laughter was constant, and they tried hard to let us in on their jokes.

As night fell, we turned onto the more northern of the two roads going west. The land became a vast, dry grassland, and the road turned into a series of parallel dirt tracks cutting across the plateau. The trucks fanned out, as each driver chose his own path. It was like a race through the desert darkness—five trucks weaving in and out, sometimes right next to each other, other times hundreds of feet apart, all of them raising a cloud of dust.

We are now parked in the middle of nowhere. The trucks are arranged in a circle, like covered wagons, and we're all sitting in the center, drinking tea and eating *tsampa* by the glow of the headlights. Tonight, Per and I will sleep underneath our truck.

The stars are breathtaking.

September 15

I slept well last night but got a rude awakening early when the driver yelled he was about to start the engine. We got out of the way just in time, or we'd have been covered in black exhaust. Our convoy joined two others, and we now have a caravan of sixteen vehicles. What a sight it is to have a line of trucks as far as you can see barreling through the dusty hills.

We drove past brilliant blue lakes so still that the reflections they held were like giant photographs. Further on we bounced by a geyser shooting a fountain of water and huge plumes of steam into the air. It was surrounded by hundreds of smaller steam vents and pools trickling down into the river. I could see the white canvas and black yak-hair tents of the nomads everywhere, and the land was dotted with their grazing yaks.

September 16

The weather here is amazing. Within the space of fifteen minutes it can rain, clear up, hail viciously, and clear again. Today snow suddenly started blowing through the cab of the truck. Five minutes later it was gone. Strange cloud formations make the landscape seem unreal and eerie.

We are now passing through an arid mountainous desert full of gravel and sand. It looks like the bottom of a great sea, as indeed it once was. The wind is intense and raises huge clouds of dust.

We've been living mostly on *tsampa*, and I've really grown to like the stuff. Sometimes we prepare a deluxe version with milk powder and raisins. Once we get to Ali, we may experiment by adding butter, eggs and sugar. Then it will be just like raw cookie dough.

September 17 Gerzê

We arrived in Gerzê yesterday evening, and who knows when we'll leave. We haven't had any luck finding another ride the last 300 miles to Ali, even though there must be thirty or forty trucks in town.

Gerzê is really the end of the world. It is situated in the middle of an empty desert, and I can't imagine why anyone ever stopped to build a town here. Except for a few nondescript Chinese concrete buildings, all the walls and houses are made from mud bricks and everything— the houses, the road, even the surrounding countryside—is the same light brown color. Beyond the town, emptiness stretches to the horizon.

The street and alleyways are dusty and littered with every sort of rubbish. Bottles, cans, plastic, and paper are mixed with animal carcasses, old clothes, bones, furs, and animal and human feces. The *drokpas*, the Tibetan nomads, have their tents set up on the outskirts of town. They have dark faces, braid their long hair, and wear heavy sheepskin robes. They drive their herds of sheep or yaks down the street by throwing rocks at them.

But the most colorful people in town, as always, are the Khampas from eastern Tibet. They travel all over the country to trade and have set up their tents on the main street to display the clothes, jewelry, and other goods they've brought from Lhasa or Shigatse. There's always a lot of action around their tents: the townspeople and nomads checking out all the wares, bargaining and bartering, music playing, and tea being brewed on open fires.

The hotel we're staying in has no facilities except a well for water. The rooms are tiny with three or four hard beds in each one. The floor is dirt and the walls are covered with newspapers. A bare light bulb hangs from the ceiling. The Chinese women who work at the hotel are quite hostile, but everyone else seems friendly.

The sun is fierce here. There is little wind, and away from the trading tents the only sound that breaks the hot desert silence is the swooshing from the wings of the huge black ravens circling overhead.

Later

Today I need some time alone. I suddenly feel overwhelmed by a melancholy sadness. It isn't depression, but rather a sense that life is not a game, that it is not just an adventure. I feel a kind of quiet urgency. At times like this I naturally turn toward solitude and meditation.

September 20 Ali

We finally made it out of Gerzê in the back of a big truck and have been joined by a Frenchman named Pascal. We found him standing alone in the middle of the feature-less desert, wearing a black Tibetan coat, a white French scarf, and a Three Musketeer-style hat. He was looking at a map as though he was lost in a big city.

The three of us got a ride that nearly shook our fillings loose. We were constantly thrown about in a cloud of dust and were airborne half the time. Luckily, the truck was filled with bags of clothes and cushions, so we could surround ourselves with soft padding and not get bruised too badly.

The truck let us off at a cluster of mud buildings called Tsaca where we spent the night in a dingy hotel with a group of Khampa traders. In the morning they slaughtered a sheep by suffocating it in the yard out front.

We all got a ride to Ali that day—the Khampas and their truckload of trading goods, some nomads and Tibetan businessmen, Per, Pascal, and I. There were

Truck ride out of Gerzê

eighteen of us plus all our gear. The goods were piled high above the sides of the truck, and we clung to the ropes which tied everything down. High above the road, we bounced along in the bright sunshine.

After a couple of hours, we stopped near a stream for lunch and everyone separated into different groups. The truck drivers, who make a lot of money and are quite arrogant, ate alone. The Tibetan businessmen from Lhasa and the Khampas sat together. They shared a leg of the sheep the Khampas had killed that morning, slicing off chunks with long daggers and eating the meat raw. The *drokpas*, a shy, naive country people, seemed to be looked down upon by the flashy, worldly Khampas and sat apart. We didn't fit in anywhere.

Later, we enjoyed a beautiful sunset that was reflected in the river to our left and lit up the sandstone cliffs to our right. It was late at night when we finally pulled into Ali. The town is situated on the Indus River and acts as the Chinese administrative headquarters for the whole

western region. The Chinese call the town Shiquanhe.
Lots of trading goes on here, and there is even a department store. It's not exactly Macy's, but it is better stocked
than anything we've seen since Lhasa.

Yesterday we began our preparations for the trip to
Mt. Kailas. We are three now, as Pascal wants to join us.
We have decided to ride the 200 miles to Kailas on
bicycles. From there we plan to return to Shigatse by
riding along the little-used southern road which paral-
lels the Himalayas.

We wrote out a long shopping list of equipment and
supplies we need to stock up on before we head into the
countryside. First we had to buy bicycles, but the store
only sold them unassembled. Every nut, bolt, spoke, and
gear was loose and separate. Our problem was compounded
when the clerks refused to open the crates to let us see
what we were buying—not to mention that we had no idea
how to put them together. We spent the entire day
looking for a mechanic who could assemble the bikes for
us in a reasonable amount of time for a reasonable fee.

After exhausting, frustrating attempts to explain
what we wanted, we finally found a trustworthy fellow to
do the job. In the basement of the department store, the
four of us opened the crates and spread the pieces all over
the floor. Then we carefully counted every spoke and bolt
to make sure all the parts were there. When the mechanic
was finally satisfied that there were enough parts to make
three bikes, we packed the small pieces into our backpacks,
slung the frames, rims and tires over our shoulders, and
carried everything to his house. They should be ready in
two days.

September 21

This morning the manager of our dirty little hotel refused to give us a thermos of boiled water, which is standard in most Chinese hotels. So we refused to pay for the room. After a long standoff he finally brought the water. We then paid, and now he seems to like us better. But the Chinese guy who runs the restaurant is still being surly. We asked him, in Chinese, for *baozi* (stuffed dumplings), and he yelled back at the top of his voice, "*Mei you! Mei you!*" ("don't have! don't have!"). Even when we ordered rice, he yelled at us and only reluctantly made the order.

September 22

Yesterday was crazy. We had been the only foreigners in town, and then suddenly everyone from Lhasa arrived at once. First we saw Debbie, then our Colombian friend, and then Monika, followed by an Italian we knew, then two other groups of hitchhikers, and on and on. To look and listen in some of the restaurants here in Ali, you'd think we were in Europe instead of on the Tibetan Plateau.

Debbie and Monika have decided to go with us to Mt. Kailas, and I'm looking forward to their company. Today, while they went to buy bikes, Per, Pascal, and I completed most of our provision shopping: raisins, almonds, milk powder, yak butter, *tsampa*, chocolate, tools, bicycle pump, spare bike parts, cooking pot. We had a tailor make us some cloth sacks to carry everything in.

We also got our bikes from the mechanic and have been adjusting, tightening, and arranging our packs all morning. There are just a few more things we need from the department store, but it's been closed all day.

Later

Wandering around Ali this afternoon, I ended up
at a Muslim slaughter tent on the outskirts of town. I
watched while the dark-skinned, white-capped grim
reaper of goats entered the small corral that was packed
with fear-crazed animals. He casually pushed his way
through the mass while the goats cowered, bayed, and
struggled to get out of his way. When he decided that
the karmic allotment of life for a certain beast was used
up, he grabbed its horns and dragged the kicking,
screaming, bug-eyed animal to a nearby pit, slit its neck,
and simply walked away. The goat choked as blood
poured from its throat, then staggered and collapsed.

One minute there was a living being and the next
minute there was only a pile of inert matter. I stood there,
staring at the carcass, and knew my inability to fully
understand death was the cause of my inability to fully
understand life.

September 23

The department store finally opened yesterday
evening, and we bought our last supplies. Our Chinese
bikes feel as if they're made of lead, and even before we
loaded them, it required both arms to lift them. They have
sturdy fenders and metal rod brakes. The tires are nice and
fat with thick treads. We don't have to worry about
delicate gear systems with these babies. They have only a
single gear which is comparable to fourth or fifth on an
American ten-speed and it has lots of resistance. They
don't have lights, but they do have bells. Rrringgg,
rrringgg.

Each of us has our own homemade pannier design. Pascal attached a wooden plank across his rack to tie his backpack to and has three small, plastic Chinese handbags as front and back panniers. Per built a saddle-like rack for his bike out of wood and cloth strapping. His backpack hangs on one side and a Chinese suitcase hangs on the other. Debbie bought some beautiful material and had it made into saddle bags at the tailor's. She lined them with cardboard to make them stiff, but secretly I doubt they will hold up for very long. Monika is just tying all her stuff haphazardly to the frame.

I've got my big sleeping bag attached to my handlebars, my tent tied to the frame, and my backpack fastened to a metal rod extending back from the rack. I made a shelf out of some wire and metal I found in the junkyard. It hangs on one side of the back wheel and holds my daypack as a pannier. A Chinese handbag hangs on the other side.

We've bought up and used every last yard of green cloth strapping available in this town to hold it all together. We're carrying everything we currently own.

In addition to the contraptions we've rigged up as panniers, we are also hauling a set of full-size tools. In Ali, if you want a wrench, you can choose between a big wrench and a <u>really</u> big wrench. If you want a screwdriver, a heavy one with a wooden handle is the only kind available. And it's too bad I sold my light, travel-size bike pump back in Dejing because all we could buy here was a full-size monster, two inches in diameter, made out of heavy steel with big wooden handles and little metal feet that fold out to stand on. It weighs at least five pounds and comes with a strap so you can sling it on your back like a rifle. Pascal has been assigned to carry the pump, as he will most likely be bringing up the rear.

Our clothing is a thrown-together collection of Chinese synthetics, Tibetan wool and fur, and various Western pieces we've bought or traded for along the way. Nearly all the clothing I originally brought from home has already worn out. My bicycling outfit consists of two shirts (the outer one is a red and white striped Danish soccer jersey), navy sweatpants under a pair of yellow shorts, heavy Army boots (I left my new Tibetan boots in the back of a truck by mistake), a bandana, and a wide-brimmed felt hat.

Last but not least, we each have a prayer flag of a different color hanging somewhere on our bikes. Mine is on a six-foot antenna sticking up from my back wheel. Now we're ready for Kailas.

Me in my bicycling outfit with Per

September 24

We didn't leave Ali until 3:00 yesterday afternoon. Per and I were itching to get back into the countryside and away from the city, but we had to wait for Pascal to finish fiddling with his packs. Debbie and Monika weren't ready even then, so we agreed to go a short way out of town and wait for them there.

We stopped about 15 miles outside of Ali and camped in the middle of a desert valley next to a stream. It was so cold last night that our water bottles froze solid. Luckily lots of wood had been washed down by the stream, and we had a roaring fire late into the evening. I decided to sleep outside and was plenty warm with my two sleeping bags, as well as all my clothes and my down jacket. Now the sun is hot, and it's pleasant to walk barefoot in the sand. The desert is peaceful—open and quiet. We're surrounded by mountains and sand dunes the size of mountains. Geese and golden eagles fly high above our heads.

Debbie and her bicycle

September 25

The "girls," as they call themselves, were supposed to meet us around noon yesterday, and when they hadn't come by 4:00, Per decided to go back and get them. Pascal and I spent a leisurely afternoon in the sun waiting. We studied Tibetan from a language book I have and were visited by two Chinese army idiots who climbed out of their jeeps and threw hand grenades into the river just to watch the explosion.

Deb and Monika were rather surprised when Per showed up at their hotel room. They had gotten blasted partying with a German they knew and figured we would just leave without them. They were no more ready to go than they had been the day before, so Per hustled them into a flurry of packing and got them going within an hour. The three of them rode in to the campsite at about 9:00. We forgave them for the delay when we saw all the fresh vegetables they had brought, and we soon had a great stew for dinner, cooked over the open fire.

Today we were on the road by late morning. The road is hell. It's nearly indistinguishable from the surrounding desert, and we have to drag our heavy bicycles through long stretches of soft sand. We eventually learned how to find hard-packed sections, dodge potholes and sand pits, and use rocks for traction. With all this sand our bikes do a lot of skidding and fish-tailing.

Monika's bike looks and sounds like a gypsy wagon, complete with clanging bottles, pots, and cups dangling from the back.

Monika's bike, Debbie and Per

September 26

I curse the road when it fights me every inch of the way. I curse the wind when it blows sand in my face with such force that it's all I can do to stay upright on the bike. I curse the gas pains I get every afternoon from exercising at this altitude. The girls are turning out to be slow and impractical. Per and I waited two hours this morning for them to get ready and we didn't leave until almost noon. At this rate it will take weeks to reach Kailas, and the weather gets colder every day.

Later

It would be difficult to exaggerate how desolate the landscape is here. It's empty and barren, monochromatic and stark. The valley floor is featureless except for the occasional blue stream or still lake, and from here, the surrounding mountains look like impenetrable walls. I feel like I'm on the moon or Mars, not the warm, teeming planet called Earth. Lunchtime presents an absurd picture, as we spread out a colorful blanket and have a picnic in the middle of this wasteland.

Picnic in the middle of the Tibetan desert

September 27

The night before last we arrived exhausted at an intersection and found a three-room roadhouse. It was the first building we'd seen in two days. We were warmly received and given butter tea, and the proprietors said we could spend the night on the floor of an empty room. Later on, we were joined by a group of nomads who were waiting for a ride to Ali, and a monk and two Buddhist nuns returning from a pilgrimage at Mt. Kailas. Our bikes were a source of endless curiosity for them. Some of the nomads had never ridden one before and could hardly manage when they attempted it. They talked to mine as if it were a horse. "Giddy-up, giddy-up." The *drokpa* women collapsed in fits of laughter.

The people at the house never asked us for money, so the next morning we gave each of them a picture of the Dalai Lama. I also gave one to the monk, and he gave me some small red pills and a mixture of four different powders that are holy tonics. It was an honor to receive them.

Pascal exhausted after a hard day of cycling

Pilgrims on their way to Kailas are always revered, which is the reason people treat us with such generosity. But with our curious clothes and crazy bicycles, we must be the wildest band of pilgrims they've ever seen.

September 28   Namru

We spent the last two nights camping in beautiful locations, but we're always completely exhausted and are only making 20 to 25 miles a day. The roads are confusing and criss-cross through the desert. Yesterday we bypassed a main town without knowing it. Today was especially difficult. A stiff, freezing wind blew all day. Worse, four of us are sick. Pascal and I have bad stomach aches, diarrhea, and absolutely no energy. Debbie and Monika feel only slightly better. Per, however, is 100% well.

Sometimes it seems this body of mine is just a burden. I keep reminding myself that the Buddha taught that our bodies and minds are *anatta*: empty of any real self or soul, simply physical and mental elements continuously grouping and disbanding, following the impersonal laws of nature. It is my mind, moved by the desire to reach Kailas, that continues to drag my sick body forward.

Today we plodded along, pushing our bikes through the sand, step by step, until we came to Namru, a small group of mud brick buildings. A few old people and a bunch of young children came out to greet us. Everyone else was working in the fields. When they heard we were going to the holy mountain, a friendly old couple gave us butter tea and replenished our *tsampa* supply. We also traded some Dalai Lama pictures for dried cheese, a stroke of luck since our food supply was running low. It would have been impossible to carry all the food we needed for the entire trip, and we had counted on buying supplies from the locals. But in western Tibet, even basic foods, such as *tsampa*, noodles, and butter, are much scarcer than

Per and his bike

Bicycling on a typical road in western Tibet

they are in the eastern part of the country. The landscape
and climate here are hostile to agriculture, and the population is sparse.

The kids in this town have big, bright, curious eyes,
and the old people are energetic and comical. It is the job
of the two oldest to keep the birds away from the harvested barley. The old woman struts around the piles of
barley and lets out a variety of whoops, yells, and caws.
The old man follows her and beats on an empty gas can
with a sheep's horn. He let me beat on his can for a while.

September 29

The old man was up early this morning beating on
his can, and the old woman invited us into her warm yak
hair tent to eat our *tsampa*. She had a fire going and served
us hot tea—quite a luxury on a frosty morning. She told us
she was over seventy, which is rare for Tibet. The wind,
sun, and cold weather are hard on the skin, and she had
deep lines etched on every part of her face, running in all

Beating on a can to keep the birds away from the harvested barley

directions. Her stove was simply a big tin can about one and a half feet high. It was elevated off the ground on short legs to let air circulate under it. She fed the fire almost continuously with horse and goat dung and gave it a blast of air with a goatskin bellows when the flames died down. Huddling around the fire, we thawed our fingers to make them nimble enough to kneed our *tsampa*. We offered her some almonds and raisins. She couldn't eat the nuts because she didn't have any teeth, but she loved the raisins. We left her half of what we had.

Fascinated with our colorful gear, the dozen or so townspeople came out to watch us pack and gave us a big, friendly send off. I felt almost healthy again, and cycling was actually fun this morning. There is no more sand, but now the road is filled with ripples and it's "shake, rattle, and roll."

Old woman of Namru

I'm pretty impressed with our Chinese bikes. Where else in the world can you buy a bike for $45 that will take this kind of abuse? We've ridden them over piles of scree, run them through rocky streams, and plowed them through ice and snow. Our chains look terrible, but they keep rolling on. There's only one gear, so we never have to bother with conventional shifting. When the going gets rough, we just lay our whole weight onto one pedal and then the other. Don't worry about the knees. This is full body cycling.

September 30

Yesterday we only rode ten miles before Monika's chain came apart. We suspect the mechanic put the chain lock in backwards. (He had done the same with Per's and mine, but we had caught the mistake before we left Ali.) We tried to repair the chain with a piece of wire, but it didn't work, and we were forced to stop for the night.

I began to re-think our situation. It was simply taking too long this way. Soon winter would set in, making Kailas and the southern route difficult, if not impossible. I brought this up with the others, and they agreed we needed to split up.

Today Debbie and Monika got a ride on a truck, while Per, Pascal, and I continued on our bikes. Soon we came to a group of nomad tents. The *drokpas* got a real kick out of seeing foreigners flying prayer flags, and they brought us delicious, warm, fresh goat's milk as a gift.

They were all wearing beautifully decorated, clean robes, which surprised us since the nomads are usually covered with dust, as are we. Then in the distance we saw two men and two women on horses decorated with fancy bridles and bright blankets riding toward us. The women and kids went out to meet them a short way from the tents and began to chant. One of the Tibetans explained to us

Monika with her packs

that we had arrived just in time to see a nomad wedding, and one of the women on horseback was the bride. The four riders circled the group of tents three times, while everyone else followed on foot. After the bride and the rest of the party dismounted, everyone cheered and then paraded into the tents where, I presume, they had a huge wedding feast. We weren't invited.

Further down the road, we ran into some truck drivers preparing their picnic lunch by a stream. They offered us some bread, fried potatoes and meat, tea, and *chang*. It was a dream come true. Our vegetables had long ago run out, and we had been surviving on two meals of *tsampa* a day and one meal of noodles with dried cheese. We had all been dreaming about supermarkets and restaurants filled with our favorite foods. Two nights ago I actually dreamt about my grandmother's kitchen, and I swear I could smell freshly baked chocolate chip cookies when I woke up.

Nomad wedding

Soon some other trucks stopped, and suddenly there was a spontaneous party by the side of the road. They kept imploring us to drink more and more *chang*. And, since this was the warmest part of the day, we also took the opportunity to take a bath in the stream. By the time the party was over, we were refreshed, content, and more than a little drunk.

We continued all day through the barren, treeless Tibetan Plateau. That any people at all live on this dusty, windswept plain is amazing. In fact, we saw no one all afternoon, only a herd of antelope, as well as the wild asses called *kiang*. The *kiang* is smaller than a horse and, with its thick neck, resembles a stripeless zebra. Golden gophers perched on their hind legs watched us ride by. They remind me of Minnesota, where I was born.

As far as we could see, there was nothing but the disappearing road, paralleled by the line of electric poles stretching on and on. We had no idea where we were.

There were no signs of any sort, so we just continued to follow the most worn-looking desert track.

Our maps of western Tibet are almost useless. Different maps locate the roads and towns in different places, and they're all wrong. Every local person we ask for directions points assuredly in a different direction, and asking for distances in kilometers is useless. The distance between Ali and Kailas is 280, according to one source, 430 kilometers according to another. Trusting in Dhamma, we don't plan our route ahead of time. We have faith that if we continue to follow this valley south we will eventually arrive at Kailas.

Late in the afternoon, we arrived at a Chinese army garrison just before suppertime. We knew their kitchens were probably stocked with vegetables, and we couldn't resist asking for some food. Per speaks Chinese fairly well, so he made a good impression on a couple of soldiers, who were wearing frilly, thin, nylon lace stockings and holding hands with each other. One of them ordered the cook to feed us, and he reluctantly made us a delicious feast. The People's Liberation Army of China picked up the tab.

Just before dark we ran into Valerie and some of our other friends from Lhasa returning from Kailas in their rented jeep. They gave us some beer, dried fruit, rice, *tsampa*, and lots of information about what to expect ahead. According to them, the "substantial" town of Moincêr is 20 or 50 kilometers (12 or 30 miles) away, depending on whom we asked, of course. And Kailas is only 70 or 110 kilometers! We had no idea we were so close. Even if we have to ride our bikes the whole way, we can be at Kailas in just a few days.

Tonight we're camped in a grassy valley filled with nomad tents, yaks, horses, sheep, and vicious guard dogs.

October 1

It's getting late in the year. When we wake up in the morning, we are covered with frost, and our water bottles are frozen solid. Pulling down my pants for calls of nature is true asceticism. Today, we climbed straight from our sleeping bags and onto our bikes to get warm.

The day began with promise and got better and better. After an early start, we stopped for breakfast near some nomad tents. Several kids and a woman with a beautiful smile came to greet us. When she saw we had only cold water for our *tsampa*, she invited us into her tent for warm butter tea.

The tent was cozy. It was about fifteen feet long and ten feet wide and was made of thickly woven brown yak hair. There were furs and carpets on the ground and a fire burned in the center. A hole in the top of the tent let the smoke out.

There was an old man inside the tent who was sewing a tiny fur jacket for a newborn baby who was wrapped up in a big, soft bundle of sheep furs. The old man was enthusiastic when he heard we were going to Kailas and wanted to make sure we walked around clockwise, the Buddhist direction, not counterclockwise like the devotees of Bon, Tibet's pre-Buddhist religion.

We gave them raisins and almonds in exchange for the tea. Then the woman gave each of us a bowl of thick, creamy, cool, slightly carbonated yogurt and offered us fresh, warm milk from a goat she had just milked. When we were done eating, I gave them a picture of the Dalai Lama, and our hostess insisted on filling my small bag with cheese and my water bottle with tea.

The Chinese forced many of these nomads into communes in the late 1960's, which radically altered their way of life and brought them great hardship. After the death of Mao in 1976, the new Chinese leaders reversed the policies of Mao's Cultural Revolution and allowed the nomads to return to their traditional system of family ownership of sheep, goats, and yaks.

We continued on. At mid-morning Per and I took a break at the crest of a hill overlooking the desert valley below and contemplated our journey. In years to come, we decided, our great adventure biking to Mt. Kailas would seem a lot more exotic than it did to us just then. We were filthy and completely exhausted, but we'd probably remember the trip as unique and exciting. It's all perceptions, we decided, and we rode on.

The endless desert valley began to break up. There were more small hills and curves in the road, and the terrain gradually got greener. The road got better, at last, and gave us a chance to get up some speed. Finally, we made it over the main pass, Chargot La, and thus ended days of gradual uphill. Now we had nothing but long, glorious, exciting downhills before us. The mountains were getting more and more jagged when suddenly we spotted huge white mountain peaks looming ahead. We stopped in our tracks and let out a yell. We're getting close.

October 2

We rode into Moincêr yesterday afternoon and found a restaurant with hot food. By the time our meal was served, it was already dark, but we decided to ride another seven miles into a side valley and visit the hot springs at Tirtapuri Monastery, which is a traditional stop on the pilgrimage to Mt. Kailas.

The night was magical. The moon was only half full, but it gave as much light as the full moon back home, and it cast an eerie glow over everything. We took a wrong turn and ended up at a house where we were greeted by a Tibetan man in a white tuxedo! He directed us back to the right path and a moment later we came upon huge plumes of steam, shining silver in the moonlight. Boiling water bubbled up from a large jacuzzi-like hole and cascaded down to a stream. There was a large *chorten* wrapped with countless prayer flags that marked the site as holy.

This morning I crawled out of my sleeping bag and walked to the springs for an early morning bath. There I found hundreds of small semi-circular pools, each one flowing down into the next, level by level. The brilliant white sulfur deposits formed rounded edges on all the pools, and, because the water temperature varied, different algae thrived in each one and created different colors—bright orange or neon green.

We spent most of the day at the hot springs, relaxing and exploring the small monastery nearby. We rode back to Moincêr for dinner and then continued on the main road until dark. Again the wind was unrelenting. Just when we felt like we couldn't go on, we stumbled onto an abandoned house. We thank our good luck that we will have a warm night's sleep protected from the elements.

October 3

A few minutes ago I came over the last pass and got my first sight of Lake Manasarovar and the pyramid-shaped peak of Mt. Kailas, 22,000 feet high. Unfortunately, I'm too exhausted to fully and properly appreciate the sight. We've been struggling uphill all day on bad roads, pushing our bikes most of the way. We've been battered by a freezing gale force wind that creates towers of swirling dust several stories high as it sweeps through the valley.

Per is far ahead with most of the food and Pascal is far behind with no food. I'll wait for him here. I'm sure he's starving, and at least I can give him some nuts and raisins.

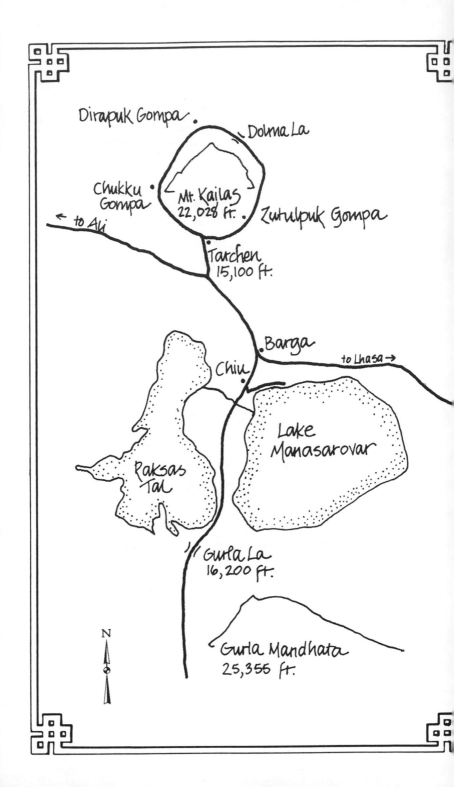

5

MOUNT KAILAS

Let me not pray to be sheltered from dangers, but to be fearless in facing them.
Let me not beg for the stilling of my pain, but for the heart to confront it.
Let me not crave in anxious fears to be saved, but hope for the patience to win my freedom.

Tagore

October 4 Tarchen

Early yesterday evening we finally reached Tarchen, a town at 15,000 feet elevation in the foothills below Mt. Kailas. At least Per and I did. Pascal somehow had difficulty finding the road and wandered, confused but undaunted, alone through the desert and finally arrived at 11:00 last night. We found Deb and Monika in a warm hotel room, and they welcomed us with hot tea.

This morning Per and I took our pitifully empty *tsampa* bag around Tarchen to fill it. We went to each door and nomad tent to trade Dalai Lama pictures for food. This way we met nearly everyone who has come here to circumambulate the holy mountain. We were invited in for tea at a number of places and were ultimately success-ful in filling our bag.

Mt. Kailas

Later On the Kora

After weeks of planning and rushing to get here, I'm now relaxing in the shadow of the king of holy peaks—Kang Rimpoche. That's the Tibetan name for Mt. Kailas. *Kang* means snow, and *rimpoche* means jewel of wisdom. I wondered if I'd feel anything special here, and already I can feel myself relaxing, my thoughts deepening. Peace is returning to my meditation.

For centuries pilgrims have come to this holy place to perform the *kora,* to circumambulate or walk the path that winds 32 miles around the base of the mountain. One circuit of the *kora* can take days, and most people do it several times. Some walk it in a single day, and a few do prostrations the entire way. Popular tradition has it that one *kora* will counteract a lifetime of bad deeds, while 108 *koras,* a holy number, will bring enlightenment.

Mt. Kailas is a place of great sanctity and power. It is located near the source of four major Asian rivers—the Sutlej, Brahmaputra, Indus, and Karnali—and is considered the center of the universe by four major religions—Hindu, Buddhist, Jain, and Bon Po. Hindus believe it is where Shiva, god of destruction and creation, resides.

Tibetan Buddhists consider it to be the abode of Demchog, a major deity, who along with his consort, Dorje Pagmo, symbolize the union of compassion and wisdom.

Debbie and Monika started on their *kora* this morning. Per, Pascal and I left our bikes at the government-run guesthouse and headed out on foot this afternoon. In spite of the cold wind, we moved steadily along the uneven, winding path with only a few other pilgrims. One young *drokpa* woman was leading a yak with a baby strapped securely on its back. The trail was lined with rock cairns left by previous pilgrims as a guide and blessing for those who followed. As we walked along the path, I could see sheep grazing on the green, grassy plains far below.

We turned north, up a valley, following the stream, and the striking south face of the holy mountain came into view. Red sandstone cliffs and spectacular pinnacles lined both sides of the valley, and its walls were covered with devout inscriptions that had been carved into the rock. We made our way past the 30-foot flagpole of Tarboche, streaming with hundreds of colorful prayer flags. It commemorates Buddha's birth, enlightenment, and death.

Then we came to what the faithful call the "Two-Legged" *chorten*, Chorten Kangnyi. The metal sun and moon shape at its very top is an ancient Tibetan symbol that represents the union of opposing forces. Holy objects sealed inside the *chorten* are said to have the power to heal, so we followed the other pilgrims beneath it to receive its blessing.

As for Mt. Kailas, I could hardly take my eyes off it. So far, we've seen the south and west faces, steep and smooth as pyramid walls, with snow clinging wherever it could—on ridges, outcroppings, and ancient sheets of ice.

Two-legged chorten at Mt. Kailas

Gray clouds at times rolled across the sky and obscured its snowy peak.

Independent Western tourists have been coming to Kailas for the last couple of years, but most of the pilgrims here now are *drokpa* families with little children and herds of yaks and sheep in tow. They bring their animals along as an act of compassion to assist the beasts in obtaining a higher rebirth in the future.

We had planned to spend the night at a monastery that was only a few hours' walk from Tarchen, but we missed the trail leading to the *gompa*, hidden in a valley off to our left. So instead, we are camping behind a boulder, semi-sheltered from the wind. I found a small cave shielded by a stone wall to sleep in and feel quite warm and content. The moon is nearly full, and it casts a beautiful blue light on the valley around us.

October 5

We're now half way around the *kora*. After our bicycle trip, the hike is not too difficult, but the altitude and weather are formidable. We're above 16,000 feet, and sometimes I find myself gasping for air.

The weather is more of a problem. Last night Pascal slept out in the open and nearly froze. A stiff wind blows most of the day. And while the warm afternoon sun can make us feel comfortable and complacent, the weather can quickly change. I was walking with a group of *drokpas* and their herds when thick clouds suddenly hid Kailas and spread all the way down to the valley floor. Then it began to snow, and I suddenly found myself surrounded by nomads, bleating sheep and huge black yaks in a heavy snowstorm, all of us heading towards a small stone monastery built into the rocky hillside.

October 6

When Per, Pascal, and I arrived at Dirapuk Gompa yesterday afternoon, we found three nomads, two monks, and two Western women huddled around a fire in a dark, smoke-filled room. The women warned us that the monks were not to be trusted. The young one, who was not a monk at all but the younger brother of the real monk, apparently had unmonklike designs on them and had flashed them that morning. The women begged us to stay. The monk and the flasher looked us over, found us acceptable, and didn't object. The monastery is a tiny place with only three or four rooms. Ours had rock walls, a dirt floor, and a thatched roof with a hole in it. It looked good to me.

We tried our hand at cooking over a yak dung fire. The night before we'd been successful using half wood and half dung, but here there was no wood and our fire was a miserable failure. The nomads watched us and shook their heads. One of them volunteered to take over and soon had a blazing fire going for our noodles. We gave him some raisins to thank him. After our meal, we went outside to watch the sunset wash Kailas in exquisite tints of pink and gold.

Suddenly another storm came tearing down the valley. This one was for real. The clouds, mist, and blowing snow turned everything gray. We could barely see the nomads setting up their tents in the valley below. They hurried around with their peculiar, bowlegged, side-to-side gait, joking and laughing, and seemed unperturbed by the blizzard-like conditions. We headed back inside, and I was glad we had a room and yak dung fire to retreat to.

North face of Mt. Kailas and Dirapuk monastery

Most of these *gompas* were destroyed by the Chinese during the Cultural Revolution, and pilgrimages were strictly forbidden. But in the last ten years, the Chinese have not only allowed, but have tacitly encouraged religious activities at certain historic holy places, including Kailas. They're rebuilding the monasteries they ruined at these locations in order to attract more tourists—and their money. I don't know if this particular *gompa* was built with Chinese *yuan* or by the contributions of pilgrims. It couldn't have cost much in any currency.

Debbie and Monika joined us later last night. They had spent the night before at the first *gompa*, which they said was much bigger. Debbie was feeling ill, and we couldn't convince her to eat anything.

When we woke up this morning, the sky was clear, and everything was brilliant white with snow. The north face of Kailas glowed in the morning sun, and its huge wall of rock and ice dwarfed our tiny monastery. We decided to stay here for the day. Pascal ran around madly taking pictures of everything, while Per and I climbed to the base of the mountain.

Distances are deceiving when the air is so clear and it took us a while to reach the mountain. We were also pushing 17,000 feet and towards the end had to stop every twenty feet or so to catch our breath. We came upon a pale blue glacier, huge ice sculptures shaped like shark's fins, and a deep crevice that looked fatal.

When we finally reached the wall, I was struck by its gigantic proportions. Kailas is small by Himalayan standards, but its sheer face rises in icy splendor 5000 feet straight up. It was easy to see how this mountain had spawned religious legends and inspired tales of magic for

Tibetan and Hindu worshippers. We, too, felt its power. It would be sacrilege to scale its walls, and no mortal has ever stood on its summit.

Tonight there is a full moon so bright it is almost blinding. The north face of Kailas shimmers with a blue glow, while nomad campfires twinkle in the valley below.

October 8

Yesterday we said goodbye to Monika and Debbie. Debbie is still very sick, and they are going to return to Tarchen. We set out early for the third *gompa*, on the other side of Dolma La pass, the *kora's* highpoint at 18,600 feet.

I went ahead of the others, and after several hours of arduous walking, I neared the top of the pass. I was gasping for air and had to stop after each step to catch my breath. While I was resting, a young nomad girl rushed past me, chasing her yaks up the slope. I struggled on.

I arrived at Dolma La alone in the midst of a blowing snowstorm. It had taken me nearly eight hours to go four miles. Soon a few pilgrims joined me, and together we waited for the storm to pass. Tibetan Buddhists believe they are spiritually reborn here and that the bad deeds of the past are forgiven by the mercy of Dolma, the goddess of compassion and one of the most beloved Tibetan deities. As for me, I just felt exhausted.

The storm stopped briefly, and it grew hauntingly quiet. Now I could see the prayer flags that covered the huge boulder marking the pass, and I hung mine among them. Tradition demands that each pilgrim leave something personal behind. Tibetans often cut off a lock of hair or piece of clothing to leave as an offering. Lumps of butter, Chinese money, and dozens of teeth, left by the faithful, were jammed into the cracks of the large rock.

In spite of the snow, the descent down the other side was not difficult. The landscape was gentler, and, after an hour of walking, the path leveled out into a river valley. I arrived ahead of the others at Zutulpuk Gompa just as the sun was setting. Unlike the last *gompa*, this one feels like a real monastery—peaceful, quiet, and reverent. The word *gompa* means place of meditation.

According to legend, this *gompa* was built over the meditation cave of the Buddhist poet and saint Milarepa. Eight centuries ago, the story goes, Milarepa won a race to the summit of Mt. Kailas against the Bon Po high priest. The priest was so surprised at Milarepa's miraculous victory, that he dropped his magic drum which fell down the south side of the mountain and carved the deep vertical groove that can still be seen today. By winning the race, Milarepa won the area for Buddhism.

I got up early this morning to meditate in the shrine room. After so much running around, how peaceful it was to sit still and watch my body and mind relax breath by breath. When I opened my eyes, I saw ferocious beings staring down at me from the dimly-lit murals painted on the walls. Tranquil Buddha faces flickered in the lamplight. Drums, gongs, and prayer wheels hung on the beams in the dusky smoke. Renewed, I bowed and slowly left to rejoin the others.

October 9

We returned to Tarchen yesterday. To seal the merit gained by successfully completing our first *kora*, we ceremoniously walked single-file around the *chorten* at the center of town, as the Tibetans do. I'd completed the pilgrimage physically, but I knew that to develop insight, wisdom, and liberation, to simply complete the *kora*—footsteps on the outer path—was not enough. I remembered advice from the *Dhammapada*, "There is no path in the sky, and a monk must find the inner path."

Pascal and I stayed at the Tarchen gompa last night, and I fell asleep to the rhythmic sound of a monk chanting. We were on our way out this morning when an old monk with crazy, bright eyes invited us to join him in the little hallway that he had made his personal space. Soon he had a fire going for tea and *tookpa* (noodle soup). We tried to talk, and he laughed a lot, whether he understood us or not.

We found Debbie and Monika back at the guesthouse. It turns out that Debbie had refused to return to Tarchen going the "wrong" way around the mountain, even though she was extremely weak and had not eaten for days. Relying on nothing but her incredible will power, she forced herself over Dolma La, step by miserable step. What guts!

Per, Pascal and I again said good-by to the girls, as they plan to return to Lhasa. We got back on our bikes and headed for the village of Chiu, located on a channel between Lake Rakas Tal and holy Lake Manasarovar, 15 miles away.

The ride as far as Barga, a small town at the fork of the northern and southern routes to Lhasa, was delightful: good road, warm sun, and no wind. We stopped to get some tins of food at the shop, but the proprietor was out of town, and the store was closed.

We did, however, meet a German there who had a short wave radio, and he gave us the latest news from Lhasa. Apparently there was a Tibetan nationalist uprising in the city only a few days after we left. A number of monks marched, waving the Tibetan flag and shouting "Dalai Lama," in protest of Chinese rule and religious repression. They were all arrested. The Tibetans retaliated by stoning and burning the police station, and the Chinese fired into the crowd, killing between four and twenty people. The city is now full of tension and crawling with soldiers. Only a few weeks ago we were all in Lhasa, relaxing and dancing. It's hard to imagine the scene now.

From Barga the ride to Lake Manasarovar was hell: uphill, cold, and plagued by a furious head wind. We worried the whole way that we wouldn't be able to get supplies in Chiu either. Per and I arrived around sunset and found a snug cave near some hot springs across the channel from Chiu. Poor Pascal was dawdling far behind, and we took turns waiting by the road in the freezing darkness to let him know where we were camped.

October 10 Chiu

This morning was very pleasant, but now the freezing afternoon wind has begun to howl, and I'm having trouble using my fingers to write.

Our cave, however, is quite cozy. Someone supplied it with sheepskins and built a large enclosing wall, so there's an entry way and a sleeping area almost big enough for three. Every time Pascal turned over last night he hit me in the face. He complained that Per and I rolled in from the sides and nearly suffocated him. We'll try it again tonight.

Our cave is located on the zig-zag channel that runs between moon-shaped Rakas Tal, which is dark, feminine, and evil according to Tibetan mythology, and Lake

Manasarovar, shaped like the sun and represented as light, masculine, and holy. Its shores are lined with stones and prayer flags left by Tibetan Buddhists. Lake Manasarovar figures prominently in Hindu mythology, too, and Hindu pilgrims come to bathe in its holy waters.

There are bubbling hot springs a few yards from the cave, and we all had a much needed wash with the warm water. I soaked my tired feet for a long, long time. We're also using one of the outlets as a stove. We just set the pot on a rock in the boiling water until the food is cooked. With all these cooking facilities and spare time, we've been eating nonstop. We made a makeshift spaghetti dinner from cans of tomato paste and some unknown meat we bought at the shop in Chiu. We collected twigs and animal

Pascal frying bread on a stove made from a metal can

dung for fuel and prepared *chapatis,* a flat bread made with flour, salt and some butter, and fried it over a stove Pascal made out of an old metal container he found.

Outside I can hear Pascal swearing in French as the wind blows his newly washed clothes off the line and into the dirt.

October 11   Lake Manasarovar

Today, after leaving our bikes with some people at Chiu, we started the 55-mile *kora* around the lake. I had already decided not to go the full circuit with the others. I need some quiet, reflective time alone. Besides, Per and Pascal's idiosyncrasies are getting on my nerves. Pascal is absent-minded, and Per is fanatically neat and clean. So when we reached the caves on the northern shore that I'd heard about while we were in Barga, I stayed behind and they continued on without me.

I am amazed at how civilized the caves are. Stone stairways lead up to walled-in terraces of apartments with stone-framed doors and windows—a sort of primitive condominium complex. I found a vacant cave with a balcony overlooking the lake and the mountains. There is a small stone stove inside with a supply of wood and dung, a counter, a sleeping area padded with straw (a bit too short for me, so I'll sleep on the floor), and plenty of shelves and nooks for storage.

Today's weather was the best we've had since we left Lhasa. I walked barefoot along the shore of the lake and peeled off my down jacket, fur vest, wool sweater, four shirts, and three pairs of pants. I lay in ecstasy on the warm, polished flat rocks along the shore of the lake until the warmth permeated to the innermost reaches of my body.

October 12

Last night I shared dinner, canned meat and crackers, with a German fellow staying in the next cave. The two of us are the only Westerners in the cliffs, although there are a couple of Tibetan monks. The German has spent many years in Sri Lanka practicing Vipassana-style Buddhist meditation, which I studied in Thailand. He's been living in these caves for two months.

When I returned to my cave, it was dark and the wind was blowing fiercely. I lit a candle, and my little rock hovel seemed warm, sheltered, and secure. I realize now how far I've strayed from the meditative stillness I knew in Thailand. How easy it was for me to get sucked back into old habits, caught up in goals, worries, excitement, and disappointment. But here, my mind and heart are settling down, just as muddy water becomes clear when you stop stirring it.

Although I'm traveling lightly, I'm still carrying too much baggage. How ridiculous it is to think my geographic goals are so important. I wonder if I'm just wasting my time traveling this outer path. Shouldn't I be devoting myself wholeheartedly to the inner path? Often I feel in the awkward position of being half monk and half adventurer. I no longer take things like achievement, social expectations, and money seriously, but I'm still living the secular life. I'm beginning to think like a monk, yet I continue to follow old habits.

For a long time I watched the candle. When the air was still, both the flame and wick appeared steady. But when a breeze came along, the flame danced madly out of control while the wick remained unperturbed. So it is with people, I thought. When life is easy, we seem steady and sure, but when trouble arises, our apparent control is blown away and we are battered by circumstance. We all have a wick inside us; we just don't know how to find it.

Then an insect appeared, circled the flame, and dove in to its death. The fool! It occurred to me that I am not much smarter. Attracted by bright lights, how many times have I jumped into the fire and been burned? Fool!

I had a strange and sleepless night, probably because I drank caffeinated tea with the German. I lay awake with the candle flickering and stared at the religious designs that had been etched into the ceiling and walls by some unknown hand in some unknown time. I wondered how many centuries monks have been meditating in this cave— a home for those who have given up their home.

Long after I blew out the candle, I heard the sounds of some furry hamster-like rodents. They scurried around and cleaned out the crumbs from my *tsampa* bowl and ran across my head a couple of times. I shone my flashlight on them, but they just stared right back—as curious about me as I was about them. Their sounds, along with the haunting wind and echoes of crashing waves on the lake shore, kept me awake until dawn.

The beauty of the sunrise made up for my sleepless night. I sat on my balcony all morning, meditating, eating *tsampa*, and reading. It's been getting hotter and hotter, and I'm running out of clothes to shed. The sun reflects off the deep blue lake as if performing in some otherworldly laser light show. To the south, the mountain Gurla Mandhata, 26,000 feet high, seems to float in the distance, a symbol of liberation, made of earth yet unattached to it. Far more birds than people inhabit these cliffs. They call out and dart and swoop through the sky, and a few hop around on my balcony.

Later, by candlelight

I just returned from a visit with the German next door. He'd been listening to BBC broadcasts on his short wave radio. The situation in Lhasa has become ugly and more complicated. Western doctors examined the monks after they were released from prison and reported that they had been severely beaten and had broken bones, smashed up faces, and cracked ribs. There are news blackouts, curfews, and foreigners' film is being confiscated. Last, but not least, all individual travel has been suspended in Tibet. This includes Tibetans and Chinese as well as foreigners. So it seems I'm on the lam again.

It's unclear how long the ban will last, but while it does, finding any kind of truck transport will be next to impossible. Even in the tiny town of Barga, I've heard they're checking permits and passports. The Chinese expect people to stay where they are to keep the news of their atrocities from spreading. With this new twist, I don't know how or when I'll get to Nepal to meet Doug.

As the afternoon gales began, white caps and crashing waves appeared on the lake. Then the sun set and bathed the mountains and clouds on the far shore in purple and pink. Here, at Lake Manasarovar, all is peaceful.

October 13

This morning I decided to explore some of the other caves. There are a good number of them, and some are much larger and more intricate than mine. Most have a stone altar, shelves, and a sleeping area. The more sophisticated ones have a separate section for cooking, with a stove and counter space. Some have steps leading up to a walled-in porch or front yard. Usually there are inscriptions of Tibetan mantras or scriptures above the door or on flat rocks leaning against the wall. Some caves are in disrepair, and others can no longer be reached safely because crumbling cliffs have obliterated the path. I'm now sitting on the front porch of the highest cave I could get to. Looking over the edge, I can see straight down to the beach, 150 feet below. The cave itself is tiny—just big enough for a short Tibetan to sleep and meditate in.

All these caves were used by hermit monks for meditation up until the Chinese invasion. After the Chinese arrived, the monks fled, and the caves were unused for thirty years. Now only one or two monks live here year-round.

The Chinese opened this area to official tour groups several years ago, but this is the first year Westerners have been permitted to come to Lake Manasarovar in large numbers. The German told me that during the summer all the caves were occupied. So far most of the Westerners use the caves for meditation—like my German neighbor. But he also told me that some come simply for the beach. If the new travel ban is lifted, this will probably become a popular tourist destination. The sanctity will be replaced by raucous beach parties, and meditation will be replaced by a drug-induced stupor. Trash will pile up, the monks will become unfriendly, and the fresh lake water I've been drinking will become polluted. I feel lucky to see it now.

Later

The solitude here has helped me gain a clearer perspective, and I've been thinking about the lifestyle I led in high school and college, even after I first became interested in Buddhism. My heroes were Jack Kerouac and the dharma bums. I tried to match their zeal as I raced through the world devouring whatever life had to offer with a frantic intensity—while meditating on the side. I hitchhiked penniless, just to see who I'd meet. I cruised the highways in a beat-up '72 Ford LTD, filled with ideas and ideals. I lived the beatnik, pseudo-zen rhetoric of "we're all ultimately enlightened already, so anything goes." Every action was supposed to be an expression of our Buddha nature. So I could meditate being Buddha; I could get drunk being Buddha; I could even shoplift being Buddha. No problem.

I used to idolize the crazy saints and mad monks who were supposedly so enlightened they didn't need to follow ordinary standards of morality. But I see now that a foundation of moral behavior is essential if I am to seriously cultivate compassion and wisdom.

I don't have to look any further than my own behavior the last few weeks to see the truth in this. Lying to the Chinese government, forging documents, running from the police, partying all night. These things only make it more difficult to develop inner peace.

As I become more mindful, I'm beginning to see which things lead to peace and clarity and which ones don't. Looking for lasting happiness in things that don't have the ability to give it is *dukkha*. Looking for security in things that don't have the ability to give it is *dukkha*. For most people, happiness comes from possessive clinging and therefore leads to *dukkha*. I'm finally learning that true happiness comes only from letting go.

At the beginning of this trip, I wasn't sure I was ready to become a monk. In many ways, I think I needed one last, exciting journey in the outside world. But this trip has shown me that I'm more ready to make a spiritual commitment, to enter a monastery, and to devote my life to meditation, than I had ever imagined. As a monk, I can spend my time looking within, exploring the inner path.

Asian Buddhism seems right for me: living under a tree or in a hut in the forest, wearing patched robes, having few possessions, going barefoot into the village at dawn to accept whatever is offered into my bowl, eating little, sleeping little, speaking little, and ardently developing meditation. A monk or "bhikkhu" is one who has given up his home and the worldly values that go with it.

"Home-less, sweet home-less."

October 16 Chiu

I returned to the cave at the hot springs two days ago and have been waiting for Per and Pascal to complete the lake *kora*. It was hard to leave my peaceful cave by the lake, but my journey on the outer path hasn't yet been completed.

Mornings are wonderful here. The lake is calm, the sun is warm, the air is still, and birds are flitting everywhere. Ducks swim in the water while noisy flocks of pigeons scavenge the lake shore. Sea gulls hover and dive for small fish, while smaller birds wade through the shallow water on skinny legs, picking out insects with their long beaks. A variety of small chirpy birds hop into the cave. Big black ravens swoop overhead. And majestic eagles circle and search the ground for prey.

Yesterday afternoon I went up to Chiu Gompa, which is perched on a rocky hill above the town. The monastery appears to grow directly out of the surrounding rock. At one time there were eight monasteries along the lake shore. After the Cultural Revolution there were none, but five have since been rebuilt.

On the way up to the *gompa*, I met a young novice, a bright-eyed child who was eager to show me around. At the entrance a big black dog watched us with some suspicion, and as I walked past, the dirty beast bit my leg and ran away. It was a painful reminder of the unpredicta- bility of life. The novice gave me a thorough tour of the place, including the cave around which the *gompa* was built. This cave, he told me, had once been inhabited by an ancient, Buddhist saint.

While I was there, Per and Pascal finally showed up. Their *kora* had been a terrible struggle because Pascal was completely exhausted. He had even thrown up. He was pitifully thin when he left and is noticeably thinner now.

I had already decided it was time to travel on my own again. Alone, I'm more apt to submerge myself in the local culture and to meditate. Traveling, I've found, is similar to the spiritual path. No matter how good or enlightened my companions are, the path is necessarily a solitary one. No one can make my load lighter. No one can walk with me. No one can tell me when I have arrived.

Fortunately, Per now wants to go north to Kashgar, and today Pascal got a too-good-to-refuse offer from a Tibetan who wanted to buy his bike. He plans now to hitchhike the southern route to Shigatse.

Today we met an Englishman and a Swiss woman on their way to Kailas. He's a travel writer who's been tracing the pilgrimage routes of Tibet and has a map collection that makes me drool. He has over 600 maps of Tibet, including photographs of sensitive Chinese military maps—the only truly accurate ones of the region. He got these, he told me, when he was questioned by the police in some border town. They left him alone in the office, and he quickly took pictures of all the maps on the walls. I've been poring over all of them, trying to figure out what I will do next.

I still want to bicycle back toward Shigatse by the southern road. A Brazilian we met at Kailas had just come from Lhasa on that route, alone on a Chinese bike, wearing nothing warmer than a pullover sweater. He told us about a Japanese guy who made the same trip riding a horse. But only a few people go this way, which is part of its attraction. The other part is Heinrich Harrer's descriptions of its beauty in his book, *Seven Years in Tibet*.

Harrer was an Austrian mountain climber who in 1943 escaped from a British internment camp in India and traveled to Tibet. In Lhasa he was a friend and tutor to the young Dalai Lama but left the country in 1950 after the Chinese invasion. He wrote his book in 1953 "to create some understanding for a people whose will to live in peace and freedom has won so little sympathy from an indifferent world."

October 17 On the way to Burang

We all decided to go to the relatively large town of Burang about 55 miles further south to stock up on food and other supplies. Per hopes to find a northbound truck from there. He and I are bicycling, but Pascal is heading off on foot, even though we tried to convince him to wait for some sort of vehicle.

We were on the road as the sun came up over the hills, and it felt good to be back on the bike in the still air and the warm sun. Then, a couple of miles out of town, my chain broke. The lock had come off, just as Monika's had. We searched my tracks in the sand and luckily found the missing link. We used some wire to replace the chain lock and were off again. Even with these problems, we feel lucky—none of us has had a flat tire the entire trip.

We left Manasarovar behind and came to the "evil" lake, Rakas Tal. This section of road was the most hellish stretch of rocks and sand we've come across yet. The only bright spot was when a tour bus heading in the opposite direction drove past and Monika and Debbie yelled greetings out of the window. We had to scramble to collect the chocolate bars and biscuits they threw to us as they zoomed by.

We had finally finished the torturous stretch by the lake when the afternoon winds started to blow. We had thought we would make it over Gurla Pass, at 16,000 feet, before they began, but because of my breakdown and the rough road, we were caught short. Even going downhill we had to pedal with all our might just to stay upright. When the road leveled out we had to get off the bikes and push them. And it was nearly impossible going uphill with the wind straight in our faces. My bike seemed to weigh 300 pounds, and the wind made so much noise, I could barely hear myself cursing it.

I'm now sitting by the side of the road, sheltered by an old mud wall in ruins. Cycling today has really pushed my limits both physically and mentally. The land is utterly inhospitable. I look around and see desolate brown sand hills and no sign of water. The only human life is an occasional dark spot in the distance—probably a shepherd or horseman trotting across the desert. Only the distant, jagged Himalayan peaks give me a sense of something better to come.

October 18

Yesterday Per and I continued to battle our way
through the rocks until we came upon an abandoned
group of buildings. We claimed a large-roofed house that
had four different rooms—a veritable mansion. Out of the
wind, warmed by the fire, and happy to be done with the
day's cycling, we settled down to enjoy our meal of
noodles and tomato sauce.

We expected another long and difficult day today, so
we started early in the morning. The maps indicated
Burang was about 90 kilometers from Chiu, and even
though we put in a long day yesterday, we estimated that
we had only come about half the distance. We wanted to
be in Burang by tonight and figured we would have to skip
dinner and ride on after dark to make it.

From the outset our luck changed. The road was
miraculously transformed into a decent dirt track, and we
enjoyed some long downhills. After a steep, winding
descent, we came to a pretty little village that resembled
the prosperous towns of eastern Tibet. The entire valley
was cultivated. The homes were big and painted white.
And there were TREES! Not many, but after seeing
nothing but barren desert for more than a month, a single
tree next to a brook was a beautiful sight.

We continued on down through more villages,
passing more and more people on the road until suddenly,
in the valley below, we spotted a real city. We'd only been
riding a few hours and could hardly believe this was
Burang, but after asking around, it was confirmed. After
the hardest day of cycling we ever had, we had the easiest.

Since we arrived a few hours ago, we've eaten at
three different restaurants, bought goodies at nearly every

shop in town, and are now celebrating with bottles of beer. No more collecting frozen firewood, no more noodles, and no more sleeping on the cold ground. Tonight we have a warm room, water for washing, electric light, and a nice soft bed.

October 19 Burang

We stayed in bed eating and drinking until 1:30 this afternoon. Then we ventured out to try another restaurant and discovered even more shops filled with more wonderful food. We vowed to try everything edible in town. We even found a bottle of rum imported from India and have been working on that this evening—old habits die hard. The stacks of bottles and piles of empty cans have taken over an entire corner of our room.

Pascal has rejoined us. He walked half the way here, spent a cold night in the open, and got a truck ride to Burang the next day. He's still very weak and exhausted, so his participation in the debauchery has been minimal.

October 20

I've been sick all day. The rum was poison. Alcohol and high altitude are a bad combination for me. I finally got out of bed at noon and found a quiet place outside to sit next to some trees. Here I can relax, contemplate the mountains, and let the afternoon sun melt my tense muscles.

From here I have my first real glimpse of the snow-covered Himalayan chain. I'm trying to imagine what type of country and culture lies beyond the nearby pass. Nepal is only a few miles south. India is a few miles west. But the border crossings are closely guarded, and only Nepalese traders and a few Indians are permitted to use them.

It snowed several inches the last two nights. It is now too late in the season to attempt the entire southern road by bike—especially alone—so I'll have to resort to hitchhiking. Few trucks travel this route, which leads back to Shigatse and the junction with the road to Nepal, and no one can tell me how long I might have to wait for a ride. Supposedly there is only a one or two month period in the fall when the southern road, which follows the Himalayas and Brahmaputra River, is negotiable by truck at all. Before that, the rivers are impassable because of the monsoon swelling, and afterward, the road is icy and the high passes are blocked by snow.

I had hoped to be in Kathmandu for Halloween, but it's clear I won't make it. Doug is expecting me to arrive any day now, but there's no way to let him know that I won't be there for at least three more weeks.

October 21

Per left this morning on a truck going back north towards Kashgar. Pascal and I are trying to find a southbound vehicle. I got a good offer for my bike from the hotel manager, who is also the army commander for the entire Ali-Burang region. After much deliberation I decided to accept it and received all but $12 of my money back. The bike has seen a lot of wear and tear, so I am glad I can sell it while it's still working. Without the bike, it will be easier and cheaper to get a ride, but it will also limit my options once I get to Saga, 330 miles away. From there, I can either continue on toward Shigatse and the official crossing into Nepal or head south to Gyirong, a shortcut to Kathmandu with an illegal border crossing.

I visited the local *dzong* or fort this afternoon. It lies in ruins, like all the forts destroyed during the Cultural Revolution, atop the highest hill in town. It must have been immense, as the ruins themselves are like a small city.

I'm feeling pretty good today, but Pascal is now quite sick. We're the only Westerners in town, and without much else to do, the two of us have been sitting on the main street watching all the people go by.

Khampa horsemen gallop through town, and *drokpa* families wander the streets. The local women wear necklaces and headbands of silver and turquoise and coral earrings eight inches long. Some are draped in saris and have a red dot painted on their foreheads. There are many people from Nepal. Some are small, frail, and dirty, wearing black or white tunics, skullcaps, and scarves around their heads. Others look like Sherpa mountaineers, with down jackets, jeans, and sturdy hiking boots. The Kashgaris from the area north of Tibet wear beards and broad mustaches. And, for the first time anywhere, I've seen Chinese men and Tibetan women flirting with each other.

Caretaker at the hotel in Burang

There are flocks of sheep everywhere, and we can see them being dragged by the horns into restaurants for slaughter. I hate the sight, but I still eat the meat.

The Chinese service people here are friendly and helpful, very different from the rude and hostile hotel workers we encountered everywhere else. The hotel caretaker is a lovable deaf Tibetan who works himself ragged to keep the place clean and in order. He comes to our room twice a day, grunting and groaning and gesticulating, with a steaming kettle of hot water. He has a long, shaggy ponytail and an earring of knotted cord strung through a gaping hole in his ear. He likes to tell stories in his own imaginative sign language.

October 22 Near the Nepal Pass

The weather was good and I was feeling energetic, so today I began a climb to the nearby pass. I needed to test my feet to see if the blisters had finally healed. I'm also trying to keep in shape.

Walking in the warm weather was a pleasure, but after several hours of climbing, I have stopped short of the pass and am sitting in the middle of a snowfield to rest. It is intensely quiet. When there is no wind, there is no sound at all. The feeling of isolation is overpowering.

My senses feel heightened, and I am acutely aware of every sensation. Time seems to stand still. My mind is motionless. I feel a great sense of alienation. The present moment seems frighteningly cold and lonely. From this perspective the entire world is only what I can see, hear, and feel. All time, all personal and world history, is just a thought. The future and past are mere illusions. All of existence is just "this." "This here!" It seems so little. Just not enough.

As I sit in the snow writing, I can hear grasshoppers and crickets singing. I wonder why they haven't frozen.

Later

I was looking forward to plopping down on my bed at the hotel and soaking my feet, but when I got back to Burang, I came across a truck full of Khampas from Dêgê, in the east, who are going the southern route to Saga on a trading expedition with goods they bought in Lhasa. They plan to take off at 3:00 in the morning. So much for the hotel. Pascal and I will sleep in their tent and take no chances on missing the ride.

Khampa tents and horses

October 23   Back at Chiu Cave

We left Burang before dawn after a sleepless night. It was freezing and bitterly cold in the back of the truck. Getting such an early start, we thought we'd make a lot of progress, but before noon we stopped at Chiu. The driver said we were going to wait here until tomorrow for some of his friends who were doing the lake *kora*. I don't know why we had to get up so bloody early.

Pascal and I played cards in the wind and used rocks to hold the cards in place. Later the driver's friends arrived, five more Tibetan men and women, two monks, plus two foreigners! Since there were five of us already riding in the back of the truck, it will be pretty crowded. The Tibetans say it's just two or three days to Saga, but the truck is a lemon, so I'm not going to get my hopes up.

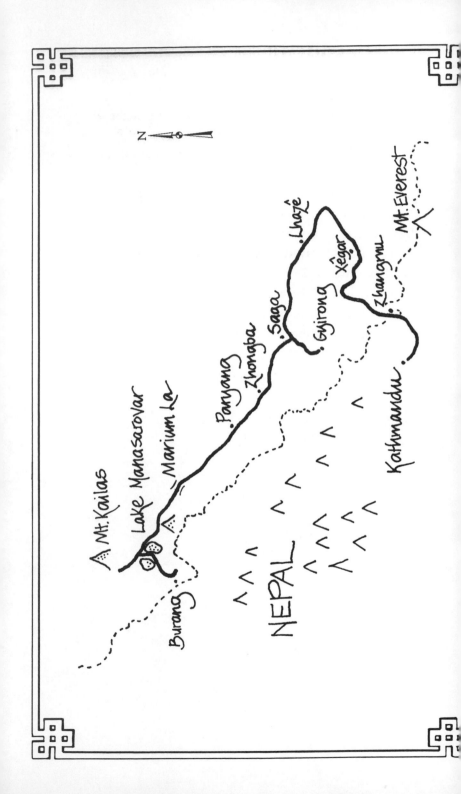

6

SOUTHERN TIBET

*If the chill never strikes to the bone, how can the fragrant
plum blossom bloom?*

Master Hua

October 24

We left at dawn. As we drove along, we saw three
wolves in the distance and many herds of *kiang* and
antelope peacefully grazing. The driver honked his horn
and laughed as the animals scattered and ran. When we
stopped for lunch, the leader of the Khampas, a petty,
arrogant man, decided all the foreigners should pay for the
ride in advance. We refused, knowing that a driver with
money in hand feels no obligation to fulfill his part of the
bargain. The Khampa responded by throwing our packs
off the truck. But we called his bluff and still refused to
pay. Eventually, he backed down.

The truck is a joke. It balks at every incline, no matter
how slight. Six times all seventeen of us had to get out and
walk. Our only consolation on this miserable journey was
a display of northern lights at dusk.

We began up the high pass in the evening—the
truck's pace was only slightly faster than walking—and we
drove late into the night. We had to walk the last half a
mile through the snow to the top of the pass. When the
truck got stuck near the top, the Khampas just set up their
tent. It's extremely cold. Pascal and I are both suffering
from dehydration and the beginning stages of hypother-
mia—body and mind are not functioning well. Hot tea

helped, but don't know where we're going to sleep tonight. The Khampas won't let us into their tent. All I can think of is warmth. This situation is insane, but the Tibetans keep laughing.

October 25

Today we began by digging out the truck. By daylight the road was nowhere to be seen. All morning we struggled over the hills of the high pass, Marium La at 16,900 feet. We had to keep getting out of the truck to lighten the load or to look for the road. Everything was snow, ice, and rock. At one stream crossing, the truck broke through the ice, and we had to haul rocks and frozen dirt to fill the stream bed and give the truck some traction. At another stream, we had to unload the truck and carry everything across the ice. I fell through once up to my thigh and had wet, freezing feet for the rest of the day.

Looking for the road in the snow along the southern route

The truck engine has serious problems; when we're not stalled or stuck, we creep along at five miles per hour. It's also clear that the drivers have never been on this road before. They continually argue about direction, landmarks, and mileage.

We're camped in the middle of a snowfield again—coldest temperatures I've felt in Tibet. They drained the radiator to get water for tea—worst tea I have ever had. My fingers barely function. It took half an hour for me to open a can of vegetables. I must continually heat my pen with a lighter for it to work. My feet are numb. I can only huddle in a ball, close my eyes, and wait for it to end.

October 26

Each day we wake wondering if the engine will start. They heat it with a gas torch. This morning we spent an hour melting snow to refill the radiator. Everything was covered with thick frost. In every direction I could see only snow and fog.

We left without breakfast and didn't stop to eat until 5:00 in the afternoon. For long periods of time we lost the road and rambled aimlessly through the snow. Got stuck in sand—had to push. Got stuck in mud—had to push. None of us is getting enough to eat or drink. I can see how people die in these situations. I can see how I could die. I don't know how much longer I can bear sleeping in the snow. I can't feel my feet. I can't stop shivering.

On the road, date unknown

Yesterday we ran out of gas. Once again the Khampas set up their tent and expected the rest of us to sleep in the snow. Luckily there were some *drokpas* nearby.

Pascal and I went over and politely asked them one by one to let us sleep in their tent. One family took a long, suspicious look at us and turned us down, but as we walked away, they called us back.

I'm sure we were the first foreigners to ever enter their tent. At first they just stared at us, but gradually we all relaxed.

For the first time in days I went to sleep with warm feet.

This morning, we returned to the truck to sit and wait. Two of the Khampas rode off on horses to find gasoline while the rest slaughtered a goat. Now they are making a bloody, gory-looking stew from the entrails.

We are fed up with the Khampas and their lousy excuse for a truck. The men yell and order us around when the truck needs to be pushed. The women senselessly shove anyone unfortunate enough to be sitting near them. To fix the engine, the drivers throw hot water on it,

Khampa woman

fiddling and tightening at random, praying to some Tibetan god that it will start. They're hopelessly incompetent. It's taken us five days, driving fifteen hours a day, to go a distance that should have taken one and a half. And we still haven't reached the first town on the map.

Pascal and I, however, are getting along very well.

Later Paryang

The men returned with a can of gas, and we left at 6:00 in the evening They tied the skinned carcass of the goat they slaughtered to the top of the cab. We went about 100 yards before the truck broke down again. While the driver played with the carburetor and made a new gasket from a cardboard box, the Khampas pounced on the opportunity to do business with the nomads camped nearby. We got rolling again at 7:00.

Pascal and I have, for the most part, resigned ourselves to this feeble truck, but the other two foreigners get more aggravated each day. They are driving themselves and everyone else crazy. Henry, a 42-year-old salesman from North Carolina, sometimes acts very dim. He got into an argument with the head Khampa over money, and they ended up pushing, kicking, and shoving each other like school boys. Henry's companion is a German woman who does nothing but complain about how awful the people are and what a terrible situation we're in. The Khampas hate them both. Pascal and I try to ignore them.

The Khampas have made a game out of pushing us to our limits. They needle, pester, and threaten us until they get a response. It's how they entertain themselves, and they're happy if you play along and do the same. I've learned that if you lose your sense of humor, you lose the game.

The scenery and wildlife, at least, offer some compensation. As the sun set tonight, it outlined the mountains in brilliant hues of orange and red. A group of yaks standing by the side of the road stared at the truck until it got close and then they took off at full speed. Their long hair almost swept the ground as they gracefully galloped away.

The Khampas sing constantly as we drive along, and tonight everyone joined in. Their songs don't seem to have any words or fixed melodies. The Khampas don't sing in unison—it's more like a collective improvisation. The men's voices rose and fell, and the leader soloed with Tarzan-like yells while the women held high notes. In unwitting counterpoint, the two monks on board began to chant, and it became a real symphony.

Khampas and their lousy excuse for a truck

Next day

The Khampas said we'd leave at 7:00 this morning, but, as usual, they weren't up until 10:00. We were all loaded up and ready to roll at noon, but then the Khampas discovered there were some *drokpas* nearby to do business with. So we had to unload everything, and they spent the rest of the afternoon selling their wares. We finally left at 4:00 and drove for one hour, then stopped at another village. Two hours later, we knew we'd be spending the night. This is the way the Khampas are. They're in no rush and consequently neither are we.

Pascal and I spent most of today relaxing in the sun and looking at the mountains while the Khampas did their business. I'm beginning to enjoy the slow journey now that we're stopping at villages and not sleeping in the middle of frozen fields of snow.

The German woman, however, is getting more and more upset. This morning she started beating on the child who has been running around the back of the truck stepping on everyone the whole trip. In the end, the kid beat her up, and gave her a bloody nose. We keep trying to explain to her that anger only begets anger, that hatred can never be overcome with hatred, but she doesn't listen.

I don't know the name of this village we're staying in now, but it's big enough to provide Pascal and me with a room for tonight. Our room has no furniture, no beds, only a dirt floor and a small stove. But after those nights in the snow it seems lavish.

We tried our hand at cooking some yak meat with our rice. We bought it from an old woman in the village, and even though she overcharged us, it was only 35 cents for a big steak. Meat in Tibet is never wrapped or cared for in any special way. It gradually dries out, and people eat it in various states of rawness. The piece we bought had hairs on it and had been sitting in the dirt and dust. We tried eating some raw, then decided to make the rest into a stew. I don't know much about cooking meat, so I just cut everything up and boiled the hell out of it. It tasted pretty good with the rice. The pieces we couldn't chew we saved to give to a dog.

Next day   Zhongba

It took two hours to register with the police in Zhongba before they'd let us have a hotel room. The German woman is crankier than ever, and even Henry can't stand to be around her anymore. In spite of that, today was a relatively pleasant day. We left at 10:00 in the morning, drove through a pretty valley, and followed the Brahmaputra River until we came to an open area with a good view of the Himalayan chain. The Khampas must have done some work on the truck. Even on the very steep inclines we didn't have to get off and walk. I am, however, suffering from a mild case of snow blindness from being exposed day after day to the intense brightness of the sun.

If all goes well, tomorrow we'll reach Saga.

Next day   Tingmay Hamlet

Well, despite good roads and a steady cruising speed of 12 miles per hour, we didn't make Saga today. The truck didn't leave until noon, and we stopped at every clump of houses and tents along the way to trade. For the last stretch we've been driving off the road to avoid the Chinese checkpoint. It's only 20 miles further to Saga, but the Tibetans are already setting up for the night. The temperature is gradually getting warmer, but I still wear my down jacket twenty-four hours a day.

Late October Saga

After stopping to trade with every *drokpa* we sighted on or off the road, we finally made it to Saga. The Khampas unloaded the Westerners just outside of town to avoid a run-in with the *Gong An*. In the end, it took us nine days to make a journey that should have taken two or three.

Pascal and I took a walk around town, but neither of us has any feeling in our feet. We both suffered frostbite from those nights of sleeping in the snow. I hope the damage isn't permanent, or walking meditation will never be the same. Pascal is going on to Shigatse with the Khampas, but I have decided to head south from here. I was sorry to see Pascal go, and I'll miss his companionship. Now I'm on my own again.

Across the river I can see the road to Gyirong—my illegal short-cut to Nepal. I wonder how much trouble I will have with the law. The Khampas were very worried about getting caught transporting foreigners. Plus, my visa is about to expire. I feel edgy here, and I'd like to leave as soon as I've washed, rested a bit, and reorganized. Saga seems unfriendly and greedy. I'll be glad to leave.

November 1

I discovered today is November 1. Halloween slipped by without my knowing it. I wonder if Doug is still waiting for me?

The town store was open and I was able to buy some good food, so I didn't have to eat at the only restaurant in town, run by a Chinese who charges foreigners double the normal price for everything. I bought cans of mandarin oranges, pineapples, curried chicken, and chocolate bars.

It was so warm and clear today that I could take off my down jacket for the first time in weeks. I joined the women down by the stream that runs through the center of town to wash my socks and hair. My socks definitely benefitted, but I'm not sure my hair did. The water was just about as dirty as my greasy mane. There are cans and rubbish everywhere, women washing clothes with detergent, and the public outhouse is only a short distance away. The stream is also the source of everyone's drinking water.

My hotel room resembles a Turkish prison cell. It has an uneven concrete floor, dirty, cracked concrete walls, and is lit by a single, hanging bare light bulb. I sit here on a metal frame cot, eating from a can of cold meat and congealed fat and drinking tea made with water from the polluted stream.

There have been lots of rumors floating around about what's going on in the rest of Tibet. Some say the entire country is closed to foreigners. Others say that only Lhasa is closed, but visits to monasteries are strictly forbidden. Today I found a poster tacked to the hotel wall. The Chinese and Tibetan versions had been ripped down, and only the English remained. It seems foreigners are still welcome as long as they don't engage in activities "incompatible with their status. Foreigners are not allowed to crowd around watching and photographing the disturbances manipulated by a few splittists and they should not do any distorted propaganda concerning disturbances which is not in agreement with the facts."

I've been gathering information on my upcoming trek to Nepal. The road to Gyirong and the border begins just on the other side of the Brahmaputra River, but there is no bridge. Yesterday I scoped out the situation and found the water far too deep and fast-flowing to ford. There is a ferry, about a forty-five minute walk upstream, but there is no guarantee the dockmen will let me cross on it.

This morning I decided to check it out. The head ferryman, a Tibetan, was quite friendly as he asked for my official papers. I showed him my Alien Travel Permit, which is no longer valid and only gives me permission to visit Mt. Kailas. He seemed satisfied and took me across in a long canoe. Of course, just because I crossed today, I can't count on doing the same tomorrow with my pack.

I've heard there's deep snow on the high passes and the road is closed so no trucks can get through. It's getting very late in the year to walk across the Himalayas. One fellow in town indicated the snow was up to a man's chest in depth. Some of the *drokpas* claimed the snow was between knee- and thigh-deep. But when I asked if the road was passable by foot, they just shook their heads and looked worried. With this warm weather, I hope some of the snow will melt.

I must leave as soon as possible. There's good weather now, but the moon is already more than half full. Although I'll need moonlight for walking at night near the border, the full moon often brings storms.

I spent the evening making Tsampa Supremes. It will be too cold in the morning when I'm camping to fix *tsampa* with my bare hands, so I'm preparing some ahead of time. When the *tsampa* balls sit overnight they become cake-like, and I filled this batch with butter, milk powder, peanuts, brown sugar, pieces of chocolate, and sweet milk tea from the tea house next door.

I'm ready to go, mentally and physically. I'll leave with the first light of morning. With a little luck I'll be in Nepal in ten days.

November 3   Busted

I crossed the river without incident and walked along the empty road for ten miles, when a jeep suddenly appeared. Partly because I was surprised, partly because I was tired and not clear-headed, but mostly because I'm an idiot, I didn't jump out of the way and hide when I first saw the car. It skidded to a halt, and I was confronted by the *Gong An* demanding to see my passport. They were wearing trench coats and reflector glasses and looked like a couple of Clint Eastwood wanna-be's. They took my passport and my pack, told me I had to walk back to Saga, and left me there in a cloud of dust.

I can hardly convey how depressed I felt. *Dukkha!* I was angry at the police and angry at myself for not taking enough precautions against getting caught. Exhausted and empty, I plodded down the road to some houses a couple of miles back and simply sat down outside one of them. Soon the entire population—maybe fifteen or twenty people—gathered around me.

This turned out to be the silver lining of an otherwise miserable cloud. I recognized a man I'd met the day before at the ferry and a friendly old man I'd stopped and talked to on the road earlier that day. Everyone had broad smiles and bright eyes. The young women couldn't stop giggling when I farted, and the men kept staring at me curiously and giving me friendly nods. I passed out sweets to the children. Each one came up in turn, wide-eyed and shy, received the candy in an outstretched hand, and hurried back to mother's apron folds.

It's these good-hearted, simple country people that I most love about Tibet. While the Khampas are flashy, arrogant and macho, the country herders and *drokpas* are humble, quietly self-assured, and proud. Their roots are deep in their Buddhist religion, and they live the virtues it teaches. The children seem happy and bright, play creative games, and rarely cry. Their parents are patient and loving, and hardly ever scold the kids. Instead the parents hold the children or play with them tirelessly. The children treat each other with equal affection.

I asked about sleeping in the village. The man I'd met the day before, Dorje was his name, showed me to his house without hesitation.

We sat around the hearth on carpets and were joined by a few of the neighbors. Dorje looked much younger than his forty-four years. He had a boyish quality and deep, sensitive, thoughtful eyes. He, like the rest of the men, had a long, black braid arranged around the top of his head. The mother's braid was woven with bright colored yarn and was tucked into the back of her apron. Almost everyone had an earring that was a turquoise stone tied to a string through one of their ears.

The mother worked with a calm, smooth, time-worn rhythm to keep the tea hot and flowing while she prepared dinner on the same fire: off with this pot, on with that one. She filled everyone's cup with tea, boiled more water, added yak dung to the fire, poured the plain tea into the butter churn, beat the milk into butter, poured it back into the kettle, stirred the coals, and put the noodles on for supper. The children ran around in homemade clothes, when they wore any clothes at all, and when the youngest child came to the mother hungry, she took a break, sat down, and bared her breast. She wore only one layer of clothing and slid off her thick *chuba* without the least hint of embarrassment.

The only modern thing in the house was a Chinese radio/cassette player. After dinner we listened to a tape of Tibetan music, which sounds like twangy Appalachian folk music. Later, we fiddled with the radio and picked up music and news broadcasts in Chinese, Nepali, Arabic, English, and even a broadcast in Tibetan from Dharamsala, the center of Tibetan culture and religion in India.

When I told Dorje of the events in Lhasa, he became very quiet. In Tibet politics go hand in hand with religion, and he seemed to be a very spiritual man. He told me of his plans to visit Dharamsala, home of the Dalai Lama, and of his great respect for his spiritual leader. Not far from the hearth, in the highest spot in the house, was the altar with framed pictures of the Dalai Lama, the Panchen Lama, and other lamas I didn't recognize displayed on top. Below the pictures were offerings of food and tea, flowers, some charm boxes, and a butter lamp that the father lit at dusk. I felt full of reverence for my host and the deep confidence he had in his religion.

There's much I can learn from this simple family. I was initially attracted to Buddhism through the intellect, appreciating the precise analysis of reality, the theory of the path leading to freedom, and logical meditation techniques. The religion of these people, however, is an integral part of their lives, completely interwoven with their daily activities. The power of such faith has carried

Tibetan Buddhism through years of vicious persecution. It can carry the faithful through the darkest of nights.

We finally retired, and I slept fully clothed in my sleeping bag on a carpet-covered cot. The others slept naked on similar cots or on the floor, covered with thick furs and wool coats.

The mother was the first one up in the morning and had the fire going before the rest of us lifted our heads. What a luxury it was to have hot tea first thing on a cold morning. Nobody seemed to be in a hurry, and we sat comfortably by the fire. Because the police had taken my backpack, I had almost nothing with me to give them to thank them for their hospitality. Then I remembered that in my money belt I had the Tibetan medicinal pills and vials of holy powders that the lama had given me on the way to Kailas. I was happy that I could at least offer them these.

Walking back to Saga, I plotted my next move. I had to try again.

I found my pack and passport at the police office in town. The police chief was Tibetan and turned out to be a decent sort. He was polite, even helpful, and didn't get upset about my visa being expired. He did, however, search my bags and confiscate the rest of my Dalai Lama pictures. Worst of all, he insisted on keeping my passport until he found transportation for me on to Shigatse.

Now I feel really defeated. There's nothing to do but wait in this unremarkable town. I keep telling myself that I may have had to turn back anyway at the pass. My host last night, whose opinion I respect, warned me that the way wasn't advisable on foot. But deep down I know I could have made it. That's what's so frustrating. I wasn't able to give it my best shot. This is truly *dukkha*.

November 4

I wrote my mother today. I don't know when or if she'll get the letter, but Saga has the first post office I've seen since I left Lhasa two months ago. It was a challenge condensing everything into a single page. Of course, I didn't mention everything that has happened.

Townspeople are so different from the country folk. They try to be worldly and sophisticated and end up being competitive and cold, not only to outsiders but to each other. They yell and hit their children for trifling matters. The children, in turn, are mean to each other.

November 5   Still waiting

I have little faith that the police will find me a ride. Trucks leave everyday for Shigatse, but they usually show up late at night and leave early in the morning when the police are nowhere to be found, and I can't leave without my passport.

This morning I found a perfect ride and went to find the police. When I told them I had found a truck, they looked at me blankly and said, "No, no trucks to Shigatse."

I said, "Yes, yes, there's one right outside."

They said, "No trucks."

It turns out the chief of police is in Shigatse, and the underlings can't or won't deal with me, so I have to wait here until the chief gets back. The deputies seem to spend most of their time preparing and drinking tea. This morning they invited me to join them. While we waited for the tea to brew, they amused themselves by looking at the diagrams of female sexual organs in the anatomy section of their police manual. By the time I returned to the hotel, of course, my ride had left.

November 6 Heading South

I had no luck finding any trucks yesterday, but when the police chief returned, he gave me my passport! Now I can try the Gyirong route again and won't take any chances this time. Once again I'm in disguise, wearing my crumpled felt hat and a beat up, torn, blue *chuba* that I got for two Dalai Lama pictures back in Chiu. I found a gunny sack to put over my backpack and have cut two slits in it for my shoulder straps.

I left town before dawn and found the ferryman in his room chanting from an oblong, unbound book of Tibetan scriptures. I was unsure if he would take me across the river a third time, but by some divine luck he did. Apparently the police neglected to tell him I wasn't supposed to be on the other side. I stopped at the house where I had spent the night, but the family was a bit apprehensive about having me around. I can understand. If I was caught staying there, they could get in much more trouble than I.

I spent a short time with my friends and have since been lying in a ditch waiting for the sun to set. I'm being very cautious this time and only traveling at night. I can hardly believe I got a second chance. I pray to the gods of Tibetan roads that I'll be lucky and clever.

November 7

I set off at dusk yesterday, figuring the last cars had passed. Even so, I walked at least 100 yards away from the road. Suddenly, as I turned a corner, there was a jeep. I was in an open area and there was no place to hide, so I simply sat down and hoped they wouldn't see me. The jeep stopped, hesitated, and then it sped straight towards me. I quickly tried to fabricate a plausible explanation for my presence. About twenty feet away from me, the jeep stopped . . . waited . . . and then drove off in another direction.

I hurried on. Soon the moon rose, one night past fullness. It was astonishingly bright, and the snow-covered mountains took on a mystical glow. It wasn't as cold as it had been, and walking kept me plenty warm.

My spirits were high, and the moon filled me with energy. I walked over a small pass, through another valley, and on to the base of the first big pass, where I've stopped. My shoulders are a bit sore from my rucksack, but my feet feel no pain. My toes and most of the bottoms of my feet are still numb from the frostbite I got ten days ago, so I can't feel the blisters I'm sure are forming.

It's late afternoon now, and I've slept fitfully here, camped up in the rocky hills. Down below I can see the *drokpas* moving their herds of yaks through the valley, and again I wait for the sun to set.

November 8

I had bad luck as I started off yesterday evening. After walking only a short distance, I twisted my ankle in some soft soil by a stream. I should have rested it, but I continued on. I took the yak trail instead of the road up to the top of the pass, and it was surprisingly easy—the beasts had plowed the path clean of snow.

As the moon rose, the wind died down, and all was quiet and light. When I came to a small frozen lake, glistening in the moonlight, I decided to camp and found a comfortable sand dune to bed down in. As I lay there with the moon fading and the sun coming up, I was filled with a great sense of well being. At Burang the present moment had seemed so little. Now it felt completely full, encompassing the world, leaving out nothing.

November 9

I became impatient waiting yesterday, and I left my safe sand dune before dark. Consequently, I wore myself out dodging vehicles. The only bright spot in that sunlit fiasco was seeing a herd of six antelope. Eventually, I found another hiding spot, and I waited there until dusk. The sunset was spectacular. Shimmering rays of red, orange, and yellow pierced the bright blue sky and shot out from the horizon like a huge starburst. The entire sky looked tie-dyed. The lake faithfully reflected this masterpiece until it faded. I interpreted this display as a good omen.

In order to avoid encountering any vehicles, I set off through a field of snow. The snow got progressively deeper, and I broke through the crust again and again. Once night fell, I rejoined the road, which was just two wheel tracks winding their way through an empty white landscape. The tracks came and went. When I lost the road, I just plowed on, mindlessly optimistic, until I found it again. The tracks were often iced over, but if the puddles weren't frozen it was even worse.

The moon rises late now, so I walked for an hour without light. It occurred to me that crossing the Himalayan Mountains in the dark, in November, alone, is a little deranged.

It was considerably colder than it had been the last few nights, and I was beginning to worry that I'd find no place out of the snow to sleep. Then I saw a light. I thought I must be hallucinating, but it turned out to be a tent. As I approached, two vicious, snarling, barking dogs came rushing toward me. My commitment to nonviolence gave way to my commitment to survival, and I kept them at bay by throwing stones at their heads. The men in the tent finally came out and protected me by kicking the dogs repeatedly.

The men were road workers on a firewood-collecting trip, and they invited me into their tent to sleep. It was warm and homey with a lantern and a wood-burning stove. I drank tea while they played a rowdy game of cards. They offered to give me a ride on their tractor to their road house in the morning.

I went to sleep content and woke up to hot tea and *tsampa*. I was feeling really good and stepped out of the tent to join the others when one of the dogs rushed over and clamped on to my ankle. It wasn't a bad bite, but it did rip a hole in my pants. Tibetan dogs are *dukkha*. To feed the dogs, the roadworkers tossed them an unskinned rabbit they'd shot.

November 10

Last night I started walking while it was still light and again cut through a field of snow to bypass the road. One out of every six steps I took broke through the crust, and I'd sink up to my thigh. I was playing a game of Russian roulette with the snow, and it demanded the utmost mindfulness. Each step needed to be slowly and carefully placed. With each step I wondered if the surface, that delicate veneer that appeared solid and dependable, would give way, once again sinking me in *dukkha*. Frustration arose. I let it go. Over and over. I walked on, step by step, one foot after the other, making my own path. I am learning nothing if not patient endurance on this trip, and for that alone my time has not been wasted.

I headed up the second pass, which made the first one look like child's play. The road switched back and forth, endlessly—up, up, way up. "Patient endurance, Jim," I repeated to myself as I plodded along. "Patient endurance." Finally I caught sight of the prayer flags fluttering eerily in the moonlight at the top. I made it! I was standing on top of the Himalayas. I felt like I was on top of the world. In gratitude, I added a stone to the pile laid in place by travelers before me.

I'm exhausted now and need to rest before continuing. Ahead of me, I can see a huge, deep valley ringed by innumerable jagged peaks. Everything but the road and the steep cliff faces is covered with snow. The road I just followed up to the pass is only one fourth the length of the road going down the other side.

Later

The road snaked all the way around the valley— hairpin turns everywhere. I walked on and on and on, but didn't seem to be getting any nearer to the valley floor. Because of the snow, I was unable to cut the switchbacks, and I was beginning to worry about where I'd sleep. I finally spotted a cave in a gully away from the road. It wasn't exactly the quality of cave I'd grown accustomed to, but at that point I could have slept almost anywhere.

Today I'm completely exhausted—sore and aching in every part of my body. I have a bad earache, and I'm afraid that means an infection. When I took off my socks, I saw the bleeding blisters I hadn't been able to feel because of the frostbite. Thankfully, it's been a warm day and I can relax a bit before I continue on down to the town below. I'm getting very skinny. My facial bones are beginning to protrude and my butt has long since disappeared.

November 12 Upper Gyirong (Dzonka)

From the cave, I continued down into the valley after sunset, planning to find a place to sleep on the outskirts of a town I could see in the distance. As I neared the town, longing for some hot tea, I stopped at a ramshackle hut inhabited by a funny old man who was half my height. He was surprised to see me, but he gave me some tea, and then, chattering the whole way, had me follow him to a tent further down the road. I thought he was taking me to meet his friends.

When I entered the tent, the smell of alcohol assaulted my nose, and a very drunk man teetered toward me waving a submachine gun. A police uniform was hanging in the corner, along with two other guns. Oh, no, I thought. Please let this be a bad dream. I willed myself to look meek and mild, and the policeman assured me he only had the gun to use against Tibetan dogs.

Underneath the drunken glaze, the policeman's eyes looked a little crazed. He gave me some tea and then offered to fix me some food. After days of eating mostly *tsampa*, I thought this sounded pretty good; besides, I was in the hands of a man with three loaded guns and was not about to argue. He proceeded to prepare a feast the likes of which couldn't be bought in a restaurant: rice, vegetables, and a mountain of lean pork. "Eat, eat," my captor kept gesturing. I gobbled it down nervously, trying not to offend him.

Finally, I convinced him I was stuffed. He put on his uniform, and, even though it was after midnight, he ordered me to accompany him into the town of Dzonka. A tractor took us to the police headquarters, where I was surrounded by Tibetan police officials.

Once again my gear was meticulously searched. They all enjoyed examining my Western gadgets and my family photos. They were quite cordial, considering they had been awakened in the middle of the night. They seemed to take more of a sporting view of my transgressions than the other police I've met. The women officials were especially compassionate and concerned about my safety in the mountains and my getting enough to eat.

Of course they took my passport. Then they gave me a nice room with a comfortable bed and plenty of tea. In the morning they brought hot water so I could wash and shave and told me I could get my meals in the communal kitchen. I am beginning to wonder if it is better to be a comfortable captive or a weary and worn free man. Where is this freedom I'm searching for?

The police are looking for a truck to take me back to Saga. I hope they are as slow about it as their comrades in Saga were. I wouldn't mind being stuck here for a few more days. The police tell me I should stay in my room, but they do nothing to enforce their rule.

Today I walked away from the sprawling Chinese barracks to the Tibetan part of town. I felt I was walking back to the middle ages. The town is a maze of narrow streets and alleys where yaks wander at will, young girls haul water on their backs, dark-faced men in black robes lead their horses, and dirty, rag-clad children playing with animal entrails dart past people gutting sheep. The animals' blood mixes with the mud and snow in the streets. High walls made of mud bricks surround each house. The doors are decorated with religious symbols, and the roofs are lined with neatly stacked rows of firewood.

The town is situated on a hill at the junction of two streams forming the Kosi River and is surrounded by irregularly shaped farming plots stretching up the valley. The valley is encircled by an array of peaks, dominated by the 20,000-foot mountain Choluhara.

Dzonka was originally built around a large monastery which now lies in ruins. However, unlike most of the monastic ruins in Tibet, which are simply dirt walls, this *gompa* looks as if it was only recently destroyed. I climbed over the crumbled back wall and made my way through the piles of rubble to get inside. Part of the second story still remains and the walls stretch up to what must have been a third or fourth story. Intricately designed pillars and lintels carved in the shapes of animal heads lie everywhere. The bright paint hasn't worn off completely, and the ceiling beams still show their patterns.

Even though many of the faces of the gods and demons have been chipped away, the murals on the wall are in relatively good condition. There are tranquil Buddhas and fierce gods who mercilessly destroy evildoers. There are depictions of the bliss of Nirvana and the horrors of Hell.

My favorite place in town is the teahouse. It is dark and dusty and has a congenial atmosphere. Here, Chinese military personnel sit and sip tea with the locals. Card and dice games are accompanied by loud wagers and boisterous drinking in the outer rooms. The inner room is for quiet, serious talks and business deals. There's a wood-

burning stove in the center where tea is always brewing.
People sit around on flat couches covered with thick,
colorful, patterned rugs. Large, ornate copper cauldrons,
urns, and butter churns, and other strange and unknown
cooking implements hang on the wall. A friendly old
woman and her two daughters are in constant, graceful
motion serving customers. As soon as I take a sip from my
cup, they come around to refill it and politely hand it back
to me. The proprietor is a hip Tibetan with long,
unbraided hair and a black leather jacket.

It is here at the teahouse that medieval Dzonka,
which is along a main trading route, meets the modern age
arriving from Nepal. Khampas in their traditional robes
confer with Nepalese dressed in tidy sweaters and slacks. I
talked to one Nepalese man who travels back and forth
between Dzonka and Kathmandu with a string of yaks,
dealing in meat, salt, and rum. He, like the rest of the
traders, had a large wad of bills, which he flashed about. I
saw one deal finalized when a man signed the contract
with his fingerprint. The whole place reminds me of the
bar scene in *Star Wars*.

Few Westerners have ever visited Dzonka, so I cause
quite a stir. The girls smile and laugh when I say, *"Tashi
delay"* ("hello"), and the kids crowd around me or tag at
my heels. A few of the little ones make tentative gestures
towards my strange blond hair as if they'd like to touch it.
The old men greet me with amused grins, but sometimes
the old women seem afraid. If I stop moving any place
outside my room, a crowd soon gathers.

I'd like to stay in Dzonka longer, but today a police
jeep pulled up in front of my room, and I suspect it's here
to whisk me off to Saga. At least they're not making me

walk back this time. I imagine the Saga police won't be too happy to see me again. Perhaps they'll just try to get me to leave their town as quickly as possible—which is exactly what I want to do.

November 13 Saga (for the third time)

I was right. The jeep was for me. This time the Saga chief of police was my escort. He got rip-roaring drunk last night with the Dzonka police chief but not before he barricaded my door with furniture to keep me from escaping during the night. Luckily he was still in a good mood today.

A police jeep is the quickest, most comfortable way to travel in Tibet: four-wheel drive, padded upholstery, even a stereo cassette player. In just a few hours, we retraced all of my labor of the past four days. As we drove by the shack of the old man who turned me in, I noticed there were *drokpa* tents just across the road. If I had stopped there, instead, I probably would not have been apprehended and would still be on my way. A simple twist of fate.

The police chief told me he has a ride lined up for me to Lhazê and onward to the Nepal border. I am being treated extremely well now, and I appreciate that.

November 14

Another boring day in Saga. The police told me there is now no ride for me to Lhazê. I may never make it to Nepal. I wonder if Doug is still waiting for me in Kathmandu; I'm three weeks late already. Folks at home are probably really worried. California seems so far away.

November 15

No trucks. Like before, the police, no matter what they say, are absolutely no help. I know they want me out of here, but they can't figure out how to get rid of me.

November 16

Again no trucks—or I should say, there are plenty of trucks, but all the drivers refuse to take me. I have found some friendly people in town to drink *chang* with, and the girls at the teahouse asked me to teach them how to dance American style.

November 17

I saw my first Westerner in almost three weeks today. This American, Rand, was in Lhasa when the police station was burned to the ground after the arrest of the protesting monks. He told me the rioting started when two Tibetan prisoners were publicly executed in Lhasa. The Tibetans claimed that the Chinese had executed them in retaliation for anti-Chinese remarks made by the Dalai Lama during his visit to the United States the week before. Rand said the Chinese are denouncing the Dalai Lama as the instigator of the unrest. It is the Dalai Lama who is trying to keep the protests nonviolent. This, despite the fact that the Chinese have killed over a million Tibetans since 1950. People in the West are unlikely to know much about these latest developments since all the foreign journalists have been expelled.

Rand spent the last two weeks partying in Lhasa with Debbie and Monika—small world.

Rand plans to go to the lower Gyirong valley and live in the woods until spring. I thought about going with him and trying a third time to cross into Nepal, but I had my doubts about whether he would make it. I also thought about Doug waiting for me in Kathmandu.

Then fate decided for me. I found a truck headed for Lhazê, 180 miles to the east. From there I may be able to get a ride to Kathmandu. The driver initially refused to take me, but I convinced a policeman to write me a "permission slip," which eventually satisfied him.

So here I sit on the steps of the hotel waiting for the driver to finish loading his truck. I won't even try to guess how long it will take to drive this stretch of road.

7

NEPAL

It is always a lonely saunter, for one always goes alone.
Only experienced men can be companions on
Nirvana's path.
By following old tradition, your spirits will be high,
But your wild manner and hardened bones will
remain—unnoticed.

Yung Chia Hsuan Ch'an,
Song of Enlightenment

November 18 Xêgar

The truck from Saga drove late into the night. It was bitter cold in the open cargo bed and was tolerable only because I was packed in with so many other people and their sheep. We didn't stop until midnight, but at least our hotel provided a warm bed and hot water. This morning we made it to Lhazê, where I thought I would once again be stuck. My Chinese money was running out, and there was no place to change travelers cheques.

But today luck was with me. I found a ride going to Zhangmu, a town at the border 210 miles away. Tonight, we're staying in a truckstop hotel outside of Xêgar, the launching point for the Mt. Everest base camp treks. I had dinner with the drivers—bread and raw meat. They are Tibetans who now live in Kathmandu and one of them speaks very good English.

There are two other foreigners in the room next door—a Swiss man, who is riding his mountain bike from Lhasa to Kathmandu, and his English girlfriend. I met her when she came bursting out of her room wearing nothing but a full length *drokpa* sheepskin coat and brandishing a twelve-inch knife at several Tibetan men who were standing outside her window. "You stay away from my window, you bloody bastards, or I'll stick this knife in you," she shouted. Apparently, the Tibetans had been spying on the pair making love.

November 20

We left Xêgar yesterday at 5:00 in the freezing morning darkness (we were still over 13,000 feet). There was a checkpoint just outside of town, and I had to walk more than a mile around it and wait for the truck there. The checkpoints are another Chinese Catch 22. The Chinese want all foreigners out of Tibet, yet they fine the truck drivers if they are caught taking us. The Chinese specialize in zen koan bureaucracy. If there is any meaning to be found in their methods, it is beyond the scope of the rational mind.

Although I was riding in the cab, it was still agonizingly cold. I have some feeling in my feet again, but I wish I didn't. Every time we stopped, I got out of the truck and jumped in place, trying to keep some circulation going so the damage from the frostbite wouldn't get worse.

At sunrise we passed through the village of Tingri. Across the vast plain, we had a view of the Himalayas, and I could see Mt. Everest. Tibetan houses and ruins of others were silhouetted in the golden light, bathing the mountains. Everything was covered with snow and a misty haze that reminded me of the gaudy airbrush paintings on surfer vans back home. It was almost unreal.

We stopped at a teahouse where an old woman served us cup after cup of steaming hot butter tea while we sat around the fire. Later, we drove over the last and highest pass, at an elevation of 17,100 feet, and had a fantastic view of the mountains to the south and east. At the top we celebrated with a snowball fight, and the drivers tied a long string of colorful prayer flags to the markers.

Soon we were below the snowline, and after the town of Nyalam things really began to change. Down, down, down we went through a beautiful steep valley. First there were bushes, then a tree, then a whole forest of evergreens interspersed with green meadows. Down, down, down we wound our way through a gorge next to a rushing river—traveling, as Peter Matthiessen wrote in *The Snow Leopard*, "against the seasons." Winter became late autumn, then fall, and finally summer. We got to Zhangmu in the afternoon, and there my ride ended.

I carried my bags down through town and was soon soaked in sweat. My three pairs of pants and five shirts were stifling. I bumped into Hans, a German fellow I'd met at Kailas, and we continued on together. Hans had news from Lhasa, where the Chinese are doing everything they can to clear Tibet of tourists. All the monasteries and other sights of interest have been closed, and officials are making life difficult for independent travelers. According to him, there are fewer than a dozen foreigners left in all Tibet, including the two of us.

The Chinese officials at the border weren't terribly bothered that my visa had expired three weeks before. They just gave me an extension and sent us on our way.

We walked another five miles to the Friendship Bridge, which crosses over a narrow gorge into Nepal, and another mile past that to the Nepali customs at Kodari. There we had our first *dahl baht* (rice, lentils, and vegetables) for dinner. Then we walked a mile to Tatopani where we'd heard there were some hot springs. The further down the valley we went, the steamier and more tropical it became. The elevation here was only about 1,000 feet.

We arrived in town just after dark, found a bed, and headed straight for the hot springs. The water poured out of pipes embedded in the rock wall like a shower and was the perfect temperature. After two and a half months of almost never taking off my clothes, I finally shed them all and melted into a stream of hot water. It had been -30 degrees centigrade when I got up that morning. But there I was bathing out-of-doors. It was all happening so quickly.

November 21 Kathmandu

Yesterday we got an early truck ride 15 miles to Barabise, where crowds of people hustled around the marketplace in colorful clothes. Cars and Mercedes Benz trucks honked their way through the congested streets. Shops were filled with innumerable items for sale. And the sounds and smells coming from the houses were entirely different from those of Tibet.

We walked two miles to where a landslide had blocked the road. On the other side we found a taxi. We gave the driver all the rupees we had, which wasn't much, and he agreed to drive us the last 50 miles to Kathmandu.

After thousands of miles of dusty, freezing, bone-jolting rides in the back of those antique Chinese trucks, I was now in a Toyota Corolla, on a paved road, with Tina Turner blaring from the stereo speakers.

As we got closer to the city, there were traffic jams, airplanes, billboards, Gucci shirts, high heels, neon Pepsi signs, and buses with people crowded on top and hanging off the sides. Just a few days ago, I was sipping tea in a nomad tent!

When we arrived in Kathmandu, we found Western-style restaurants, pizzerias, cake shops, rock cafes, and all the foods I'd been seeing in my dreams. We found a hotel and changed some money, then ate and shopped our way through town. Cakes, lasagna, chocolate bars, fruit milk shakes, and brownies—we bought anything that looked good. I finally found light-weight shoes to replace my heavy boots and bought a new pair of pants to replace my filthy, torn green ones.

There were letters from home at the American Express office, and I read them hungrily. I also had a note from Doug. He waited a month for me in Kathmandu and then sent a telegram to my mother asking where I was. She probably thinks I'm dead. Doug is now on his way to India. I missed him by just one day!

November 22

I'm feeling a little sad about leaving Tibet. I loved the people and the adventure, but the continual cold was hard to endure. The luxuries of Nepal have made me remember that you get no points for simply suffering.

When I was back in Saga, Rand told me I looked pretty "weathered." When I saw myself in a mirror again,

I saw a few new lines on my face. The toes and soles of my feet are still numb except for the shooting pains I often get. The ankle I twisted doesn't hurt anymore, but it is very swollen. My legs are skinny, though wiry and solid. Most of my skin is a sickly white color, but my hands resemble my boots—black, dry, dirty, and cracked. They look as if they belong to someone twice my age. And my eyes still sting a bit from the snow blindness.

I am very thin. I really noticed it in the shower yesterday. I was skinny when I went left Thailand for China, and I've probably lost ten pounds since then. Gaining weight will be the most enjoyable part of my recovery. It won't be long, I'm sure, before all my physical souvenirs from Tibet will be gone.

8

IN RETROSPECT

❖

*When you can't move forward and you can't move backward and
you can't stand still, this is your place of non-abiding.*
Ajahn Chah

When I began my journey through Tibet, I kept
asking myself if the trip was simply one last orgy of
freedom and excitement. I didn't know if it would really
increase my understanding and bring me any closer to
inner peace. Looking back over what I have written, now
that I've had time to gain perspective, I can see how my
journey sharpened my decision to become a monk and
how it helped prepare me for life in the monastery.

Traveling in remote areas forced me to be constantly
alert and aware. I never knew where I would sleep, what I
would eat, or what other problems would threaten me. I
had no choice but to accept the discomforts I encountered
and to learn how to cope with them—to accept *dukkha* and
to let it go.

The bounds of my patience expanded. Things that
used to frustrate me and make me lose my temper now
merely interested me. I developed equanimity—a calm,
joyful acceptance of all things. Patient endurance eventually got me to my goal.

When I returned home to California after my trip, it
was obvious to me how modern society obsessively and
neurotically attempts to eliminate any trace of physical or
mental discomfort. Difficulties are ignored or drowned out
with sensory stimulation, alcohol, and television. But for
me, this continuous effort to run away from problems or to

pretend they didn't exist was a heavy burden, a prison. *Dukkha*.

My journey taught me to be content with few possessions and luxuries. By traveling light physically, I was able to travel light mentally. My closet full of clothes at home seemed incredibly excessive, and I knew it was time to give it all away.

In Tibet I explored the "outer path" of the world around me, motivated by physical goals and destinations. But the continual moving around, the constant hassles and excitement eventually became mere distractions. The road is a good teacher, but by the end of my journey I saw the limits of what I could learn from it.

For a while I wasn't sure if the outer path was leading me somewhere or if I was just running in circles. But then I knew it was time to STOP. "Nothing to do, nowhere to go, no one to be." Just look and see. I was ready to devote myself to traveling the "inner path" and to turn all of my mind's attention inward to watch itself.

Jim Reynolds returned to Thailand in September 1988 to ordain as a Buddhist monk.

About the Author

Jim Reynolds is a native of Minneapolis, Minnesota, and completed high school in Sharon, Massachusetts. He has a Bachelor of Arts degree in Eastern Religion from Carleton College, Northfield, Minnesota. Now known as Chandako Bhikkhu, he is presently a Buddhist monk at Wat Pah Nanachat, an international forest monastery in the northeast part of Thailand, near the Laos border.

Glossary

Tibetan Terms (unless otherwise noted)

chang barley beer

chorten religious monument containing holy relics; ranges in size from a few feet to many stories; usual shape is rectangular base with a spire.

chuba heavy robe

drokpa nomad

dzong fort

gompa monastery, literally "place of meditation"

Gong An Chinese police

jiu clear Chinese alcohol

Khampa inhabitant of eastern Tibet

kiang wild ass

la mountain pass

lama spiritual teacher who is usually also a monk

tsampa roasted barley flour

yak Tibetan ox

yuan Chinese money; worth about twenty cents in United States currency

Place Names: Tibetan/Chinese

Ali/Shiquanhe

Bomi/Zhamo

Gertse/Gerzê

Lhatse/Lhazê

Linzhi/Nyingchi

Shegar/Xêgar

Shigatse/Xigazê

Tibet/Xizang

Tsang Po/Brahmaputra River (Hindi)

Zhangmu (Chinese)/Khasa (Nepali)

Buddhist Terms

(The Pali form of the word is used with its Sankrit form appearing in brackets.)

anatta not me, not mine; not constituting a self or soul

anicca impermanence; all things rise, exist, and pass away

The Buddha founder of the Buddhist religion 2,500 years ago, "The Awakened One"

Dhamma [Dharma] nature; the path of practice in accordance with nature; the teachings of the Buddha

dukkha stress, conflict, and inability to fully satisfy; all the pain, ills, and sufferings of life

kamma [karma] intentional action which results in states of being in this and future lifetimes

mantra prayer or chant; best known in Tibetan Buddhism is *om mani padme hum*

mindfulness being aware

Nibbana [Nirvana] enlightenment; permanent, unchanging state without dukkha, the goal of Buddhist practice; the ultimate cool

Noble Eight-Fold Path steps toward enlightenment along the path of Buddhist practice: Right View, Right Thought, Right Speech, Right Action, Right Livelihood, Right Effort, Right Mindfulness, Right Concentration